FROM BREMRIDGE TO BROOKSIDE

Also by Dorinda Jeynes:

Back Along, Up Bremridge
  – A Diary of Times Remembered

Under the Hills of Bremridge

from
BREMRIDGE
to
BROOKSIDE

Dorinda Jeynes

UNITED WRITERS
Cornwall

UNITED WRITERS PUBLICATIONS LTD
Ailsa, Castle Gate, Penzance, Cornwall.

British Library Cataloguing in Publication Data:
A catalogue record for this book is
available from the British Library.

ISBN 1 85200 105 4

Printed in Great Britain by
United Writers Publications Ltd
Cornwall.

To the memory of a toad.

Contents

Introduction

This Book, *From Bremridge to Brookside* will be the last in the series. It deals with the move we had to make from Exeter to London some time after my husband was demobbed and returned to Devon after the 1939-45 war.

We enjoyed life in a quiet suburb of the big city for several years until we moved to a country district in Surrey, to a smallholding of about ten acres, part of which was let to a college for student demonstration purposes.

When this land was eventually relinquished it provided us with the opportunity of keeping large animals, although we did have a couple of years growing corn and having the thresher here – just like the ones I remembered in the courtyard at Bremridge from my childhood. The bags of 'douce' made good litter for the fowls, kept them happy for hours scratching in it for the handful of grain thrown in.

We rented other land nearby but it had to be given up when the route of the M23 was constructed. Dairy work then had to stop and John, my son, decided to 'move on'.

There are times when that road carries millions of cars, nose to tail or cheek to cheek – let one have difficulty and every vehicle on that side of the motorway has to crawl.

We hope the end of Brookside is not in sight but there are moves afoot on behalf of the Redhill Aerodrome whereby this property would become part of their domain – in fact I have been told that more than once!

1

From Bremridge to Brookside

"Has Jake been out yet?" that question was asked nearly every night and the answer usually was:

"I'll let him out in a few minutes." My stock reply.

This night it was different – I was hesitant about the black and white collie type cross-bred taking himself out for he often came back out of breath and panting, although he seemed to have enough common sense to remain in the field and not go on to the road. He endeavoured to keep pace with every car which went up or down whilst staying in the field, but you could not be sure, for Jake could jump as high as any other dog and if he knew there was a place in the hedge which could let him through without too much of a struggle he would chase cars – a dangerous occupation.

I had come in from 'shutting-up' all the poultry houses and as I came into the porch I saw an animal which always filled me with foreboding – he, for one always assumes a toad to be 'he', was coming over the mat as if he had been a visitor invited into the cottage.

My mind instantly flew back to Grandpa and the Bremridge Farm days in Devon, and the toad I had saved by allowing it to crawl away under the wood-rick out in the court; but there was the other one which was discovered in the harvest field and which Henry had killed, mercilessly stamping his heavy nailed boot into it. "They bring bad luck," was his only comment!

Whether toads can really bring bad luck and can ever be proved to be doing so I don't know, but certainly Grandpa did have his share of bad luck. Maybe it was common to most farmers in those days – perhaps we did not hear too much about it.

Years have passed since those Bremridge days and here we are at Brookside. There was the Exeter period where I had several years at St. Wilfrid's School, taught mainly by the Nuns, and Sister Edith said something which has really ruled my life. She said, "Dorinda is very thorough," and it was written on my report. Grandma was very pleased over that remark and, to be honest, when I have been tempted to 'do half a job' or 'skimp', the vision of Sister Edith pushing her spectacles up over her nose and looking at me is enough to make me take the trouble to do whatever it is properly and with the greatest of care.

There were my years in an Exeter insurance office; there was some time in Southern Command Headquarters in Salisbury; a short war-time stint at the Post Office in Plymouth and, through an exchange in the Civil Service, several years in The Forestry Commission.

I married Douglas, and remained in The Forestry Commission until my first baby, Jeyne, was born at Woodhayes Nursing Home in St. Leonards.

We lived in Exeter with Mum and Grandma. Jeyne was about seven months old when Grandma died.

There was another baby, John, born about two years later and then my husband Douglas was moved by his Civil Service employers to work in London.

We knew it would be a terrible upheaval to move ourselves up to the capital. Of course we immediately set about trying to sell 48 Old Tiverton Road, Exeter, a house we had been only too glad to buy when we were bombed out of 84 Bath Road, Exeter, during the war. This had been our first stop when we left Rose Cottage which was at Heath Bridge, below Bremridge Farm. I think I am right in remembering that we stayed in the Bungalow next to Rose Cottage for some time, could have been months, could have been a couple of years. Anyway, Heath Bridge had been home to us, both the Bungalow and the Cottage, both very comfortable, when we needed accommodation – and we made use of the Bungalow again when we were first bombed out.

We advertised '48' and there were people to view; coincidence, of course, but three different hopeful buyers all had the same surname and as far as we knew they were not related. They were

11

all called 'Williams'. In fact, even up here in Surrey people with that surname have been friends – perhaps we attract them. After all our selling arrangements for '48' fell through, Mum and I decided it would be best to let the ground floor furnished. There were already good tenants in the next floor and the attics, so the letting was put into the hands of an agent, an estate agent. Unfortunately, after a couple of years, these tenants walked off with the furniture and owing money. They went to Scotland. The advice from our solicitor was that there was nothing we could do until they came back to England, so the case was dropped.

After that Mum said it was too much bother to try to let as furnished property, so people had to be responsible only as tenants of unfurnished flats.

It was taken for granted that Mum would come with us to London and Douglas did all the searching for suitable accommodation in a suburb which was not too far out, but he would still have a train journey every day. He settled on a four-bedroomed detached house in a quiet cul-de-sac in Worcester Park.

Most of the time, all through the years, Douglas and I agreed very well together but there was one bone of contention between us – my property in Devon, and the fact that I needed to go there maybe once a year, maybe once in two years.

The house in Exeter was under the management of a very good agent. I believe he was an offshoot of the original firm who had looked after everything when we had gone to Worcester Park and Mum was in charge.

One day we had a communication from Exeter City Council with all the alterations they stipulated as being necessary for a house in multiple occupation.

I did not have anything like the money it would need, but the ECC supplied that, on a repayment basis, of course. All this was years ago and I only paid visits there about every two years.

The small property out in the country was a different matter. After the Bungalow became empty following a fairly long let I decided it would be possible to cater for summer visitors by redecorating and refurnishing.

Oh dear, oh dear, I was a 'black sheep' – "How long do you think you will be away?" "What have you got to do that no one else can?" I should have felt flattered that I was so important at home; I felt sorry for the girls and John because if things had really gone wrong they would have been 'in the firing line'.

During the early years of my trips I stayed in Sandford with Ivy (Miss Heard of The School) and her sister May, where they did their best to see that I was well looked after in the week, and then I went down to Starcross and Mrs Williams for the weekends. When electricity came to the district, I was then able to remain in the Bungalow with all the decorating paraphernalia I needed, indeed it was 'WORK'.

Going 'back home' and seeing all my old friends was all the holiday I needed and I did enjoy it, even to painting up and down the walls. I have described much of this in my previous book.

I could hardly blame Douglas for developing his own interests – he took up old time dancing and he had an elderly partner. She was invited and came to tea one Sunday afternoon here at Brookside – a very pleasant lady, but I took a dim view of it when I learned that they were going on a dancing holiday together; Scarborough or Torquay, I believe they visited both resorts over several years.

It has been a good life here at Brookside; not all roses, of course. As with any farming enterprise the weather is all important. Waiting and waiting for settled conditions before the hay is cut, worrying until it is all safely baled and stored.

The life of baby chicks hangs on a thread for some time – they will do all they can to kill themselves, even to sitting in the sun and feather picking, starting at the tail until it is raw – and that's one more that will never live to grow up and produce eggs.

Oh yes, we've had it all.

It is not every baby calf born which 'makes it' either, though most of them did. I reared a dozen or so for a young farmer, quite satisfactorily, but the blighter 'had' me in the end. It was my own fault for trusting him – well, it is all history now, and I've moved on.

As I finished feeding the pony down in the yard today and turned to come up the garden path, there it was again, a toad, a young toad not waiting for me to step over him but long on his legs and hopping across my path.

Perhaps it has all turned 'full circle'.

2
Going to London

Naturally there were all sorts of preparations and decisions to be made about going to London and Mum had to select a reliable agent to look after the affairs of the house '48 Old Tiverton Road, Exeter' so a very old established firm was selected: Rickeard & Michelmore.

I am not sure what happened to this firm over the years but eventually management was in the hands of Mr T. A. Connole of another firm.

Out at Heath Bridge Mr and Mrs Hammett were in Rose Cottage and had 'overflowed' into the Bungalow as well, as more bedroom space than the Cottage could provide was necessary for the boys and the girls. They had also made arrangements with the owner of the Brake, an extra piece of land, so that they could have at least one cow and some young stock, so there was no property worry on their account.

There had been worry on account of Mum's health since her operation in the Royal Devon & Exeter Hospital for the removal of breast cancer, which had been much delayed by extremely unfortunate circumstances – even to being ready for admission and going to the hospital, only to be told that there had been a coach accident and a bed was not available for her. Then another delay was caused because she fell and broke her arm going to the front door of '48' and slipped on a mat!

By the time we were going to London she had seemed more or less well and was quite looking forward to the move. So, on the day in question Jeyne, about five years old, young brother John,

14

well passed the toddler stage, Mum, and me with Andy Mose on a lead, for we would not consider either having him 'put down' or left behind with someone else, got ourselves to the station and were able to relax. The dog had to go into 'the van' – goods van – and we had the carriage to ourselves. It was a warm day, outside coats were soon shed and the children enjoyed their freedom.

We had all left Exeter, but to what and for what? Douglas was not on this journey with us, he had travelled on ahead so as to be ready to receive our furniture etc., on its arrival from Exeter. However, he was there at Waterloo to meet the train and take us 'home', hoping and hoping no doubt that we would like the house he had chosen. I do not remember what the financial arrangements had been but there was a mortgage – bearing no resemblance to today's prices, but then nor were the salaries, wages, rewards, or whatever you like to call 'pay for work or services'. The house was detached and with four bedrooms, in a cul-de-sac in Worcester Park. I liked the sound of that address 'Worcester Park' particularly, as I knew that my father had had some connections with Worcester in the Midlands.

Our house was not far from the railway station so, to begin with, it was not a question of standing all the way up to Waterloo. That came later and was a factor in Douglas's desire to live even further out where travelling conditions should have been more comfortable. However, here, now, we were, and a school – the nearest one – gave Jeyne her start in education. Mr Harman was the headmaster and I think his second-in-command was a Mrs Broome.

We had taken John's big perambulator with us because he was not too old or too big to be able to enjoy a ride in the afternoon for the shopping. There was quite a good selection of shops within a short walk which took you under the railway bridge and along the short stretch of pavement until you reached the busy part of the town.

It was on a shopping trip that we passed a shop with a good display of fruit and Mum started laughing, I did not see anything to laugh at, so I said, "What is the joke?"

"I'll tell you all about it when we get home," was all she said, but she was still chuckling to herself even when we reached home.

"You remember the layout of Bremridge on the way to East

Village and the 'dip' past the orchard with the stream at the bottom where in wet weather you had to pick your way gingerly over the stones. Well, above that there is a slope which borders Nannypark field. In that hedge there were – still are, I expect – two large elm trees and a little further on, on the other side of the track, there was Grandma's Oak Tree. Between these two 'landmarks' in summer there was always a sandy area which seemed to be especially attractive to sheep and lambs, a lying down place.

"Well, when Uncle John came to stay for a few days he brought his two daughters, Jenny and Polly, good sized girls. Uncle John was naughty, he told the girls that the little black 'pellets' were like black currants – good to eat, but he did stop them from being picked up, just in time."

I asked Mum what else she remembered about Uncle John. From parish records I have received from some of my good friends in Devon I believe he must have been the young member of the Stoyle family – the only one not living at Prowse – farming in Spreyton, Devon. He was quite young with an equally young wife.

In time Uncle John and his wife seem to have gone to Birmingham to live and he had a draper's shop there. It seems all went well until there was the birth of a little girl, Polly, when his wife suffered from depression to such a degree that she could not get over it and committed suicide by drowning herself.

Then, Mum said, things went from bad to worse. Uncle John appears to have married again, or at least had a relationship which was not entirely satisfactory. She is said to have taken clothes from the shop for the little girls – payment uncertain. Worse than that, she appears to have been lazy and disliked getting up in the mornings. No doubt exasperated and cross he took action. Whether it was his own goat or one he borrowed Mum did not know, but she said he took a goat upstairs to shift her out of bed! It did, but I think that was the end of the shop in Birmingham for it was known that he went to South Wales to work in the coal mines and the two little girls went with him.

Mum said that they lost touch with Uncle John, and the girls were probably too young or immature to think of writing to Uncle William or Aunt Sophie at Bremridge.

One wonders why he left Devon in the first place; perhaps the

16

farm at Spreyton became too much of a burden. I do remember Grandpa saying that he went to 'Boards School' there, along with George Lambert who became a Labour MP, I believe. Grandpa's remarks about him were somewhat disparaging, particularly as farmers were going through a very lean time towards the end of the 1920s.

With so much time passed since Mum's young Bremridge days it is no wonder that she did not remember very much more about her uncle or her cousins. I had to be satisfied with the information I had, although there were snippets of information about 'the old days' and some of the local young farmers; bright lads by the sound of it. The girls, much more ladylike and refined, seemed to have had their share of domestic duties – always directed towards the comfort of their menfolk! They were in the home, the men were in the fields with their much more important work of looking after their animals and crops. I can still remember Grandpa's hard working and primitive method of controlling 'dashiels' in the corn fields merely with the long-handled 'stabber': a piece of sharp metal about two inches long and slightly wider, mounted on a long stick and also used as a substantial walking aid through the mud, for the guiding of animals into houses, etc. No weed controlling chemicals for general use in those days. The first tractor in the district was 'a marvel'. How times have changed indeed.

To get back to life for our family in Worcester Park. It could be said to be a quiet period, and the fact that Lavinia (my wonderful sister) and her husband Derek lived in a modern house near Tolworth meant that visits were possible by using the bus, with only one change. In time I found a back way which could be walked – a very pleasant walk through several fields, although I expect that by this time they have been built over – in the Cuddington area.

Lavinia was always delighted to see me, of course. The accommodation problem had been difficult for her and Derek, they had accommodation in a friend's flat for some while and, Marilyn my niece tells me, had both queued for hours when the Hunters Road houses were to be allocated to the most needy. They had been lucky, for houses in that road were highly prized – perhaps as an ex-serviceman he had gained 'points'.

Their Marilyn was born in November 1947 – 11th! It was in

the Bearstead Nursing Home opposite Hampton Court Palace. In those days, and even when I produced my Janet, it was customary to remain in bed, or resting, for days longer than the modern mother needs to do – a wonderful few days 'off-duty' with only the new baby to be really concerned with – or about.

I know that Mum went over to Hunters Road and stayed for a few days to help Lavinia cope with her new baby and new house and that Mum felt more or less all right then. Later on that year I found that *I* was pregnant again.

It was at a routine prenatal visit to the doctor – Dr Robinson, fairly elderly but with a disability he had carried all his life; he had either suffered an accident when he was quite young or he had been born with one leg so much shorter than the other that when he stood upright one foot was about six inches off the ground (after all this time I am not sure which was the short one). Anyway, he said, "You know you will not have your mother to help you when the wee one comes, she is not at all well."

There were two or three other partners in the New Malden Road Practice so Dr Robinson was not on his own. You never knew who you were going to have to come and 'see' any ailing child and each seemed to have his own catch phrase. One always said, "Shall we have a little listen?" before prescribing the treatment, usually a bottle of quite nice tasting medicine! All the same I felt much more confident when I heard the uneven footsteps outside the front door and knew who our doctor was!

It was early in November when Dr Robinson had to be called as Mum was feeling so poorly. He came immediately and she entered St. Helier Hospital at Carshalton within a few hours. I have described in my previous book a little about the treatment – or lack of it – which she received while she was there. Suffice it to say that from then on I had a dread of having to send anyone to a hospital again.

3

Life at Worcester Park

Well, Janet Mary was born on the 18th May, 1950, a 9lb baby, and everything was so much more simple and straightforward at home than it had been in the Woodhayes Nursing Home in Exeter where the first two were 'hatched'. The nurses who came with their equipment, 'gas and air' I believe they called it, were a cheerful pair. There were no complications, but I heard a very uneven tread on the stairs next day and I knew who was coming!

Life was fairly quiet for a while after this, only domestic problems to solve and the two school children to attend to. It did not last too long, however, for one day a young gentleman called with a proposition – could we accommodate some students who were over in this country to learn English before they went on a course at Sandhurst.

Naturally I could not decide this without talking it over with my husband. Money – or the lasting lack of it – had been a bit of a problem, so he agreed. After all, we had a spare bedroom, Mum's room, and it was no good living in the past and regretting what could have been!

Our first visitor was Major Hassan, from Jordan – the Hashemite Kingdom of Jordan to be exact. He was very straight and tall and very little trouble, except that he was particularly fond of fish, 'samock' I think he called it – making movements as if to swim in the sea until I got the message.

"Now, Um John, I go to the market and I bring you samock, yes?" And so he did, a big parcel of fish left on the floor of the kitchen while I was upstairs seeing to baby Janet. It was a good

19

job that we did not possess a cat in those days!

Then came 'Mutlac' – my irreverent children kept calling him 'Mutblack'. He was much younger than Major Hassan, a lieutenant then, and really quite full of fun. He used to pick Janet up in his arms and take her round the garden, and when she began to smile it was a case of "Look, Um John, she smiles at me!" – I should think so, too, with all the weird noises he was making!

The next was Suwan 'something' I never did know how to pronounce his surname. He was quite small in stature and very hesitant when he was trying to explain something. He always seemed to be very carefully folding a handkerchief before putting it back in his pocket. I do not know how much his English improved for being with an English family – he seemed too shy to start a conversation and knew little of how to join in. I hope he did well.

For a short while there was Abdulla Majalli whose command of English was perfect – he seemed a very jolly character and could talk on many subjects.

Akash el Zabin (at least I think that is the right spelling) was with us for a short time also. Both these gentlemen went to London quite frequently.

I have forgotten his name now after all this time but King Hussein's driver was another visitor, although I was quite pleased that he did not remain with us very long because I found he carried a gun – pistol, I expect – and he had a habit of leaving it on a chest of drawers where it could have been picked up by our little boy, John, which was obviously a bad risk.

Abdulla Felaj came to us after staying with a parson and his family some way off. He had caught the parson's habit of standing in front of the fire and discussing things as if he was delivering a sermon. He was a cheerful character then but I heard later that he had refused to answer a military challenge in his own country and had been shot! The rumour could not be confirmed, of course, but it was said that he had lost his wife. I don't know.

Hani Hadadine was very proud of his family 'at home' and he carried a photo of his little boy in his pocket. He showed it to us – the poor little chap was completely naked. I said what a shame to show a child like that! Hani replied, "Shame, Um John, no, we're proud of him!"

There was another Abdulla whose nightly ritual included a foot bath.

I believe there were two 'boys' with us when something happened one afternoon. I had prepared an apple dish for tea, one of their favourites, when they came in and just looked at it and disappeared. Miss Dench, a near neighbour, walked up the road, and as she passed she said, "What have you done to your 'boys'? They are down on the seat at the bottom of the road looking as miserable as sin." What had I done?

By the time they returned later I had already heard that King Abdulla of Jordan had been murdered in his own country. We did not have television in those days but the radio reported the sad news.

Some time later Douglas and I were invited to the Jordanian Embassy in Phillimore Gardens in London – and we went and felt that it was quite an honour.

I don't think Mr Hindowi had military connections – he stayed with us for several weeks and always went out to get his train for London dressed as a businessman, complete with rolled umbrella.

Our final visitors from Jordan were a complete family who needed accommodation for a short time. Of course, I do not know why Captain Mahasna had his wife with him and his two little children, Doride and Mahassen, one a toddler and the baby very young. When they went out I offered them my 'Marmet' pram for which they were very grateful.

I suppose you could say that all these Arab boys, perhaps I should say 'gentlemen', were like ships that pass in the night, we did not hear much more from them, except one, Mutlac Eid, and he became a high ranking officer. He came to visit us after we left Worcester Park and I remember that he had two of the most handsome sons you could set eyes on but his daughter had been 'behind the door' when looks were given out for she could best be described as 'plain'. Mutlac's wife knew some English and communication with all of them was not a problem.

With my own children quite young at this time I did have some domestic help; a Mrs Jarvis came over from New Malden about three times a week. I can tell you I very much valued her assistance – and friendship – I believe she had a little girl of school age but she never spoke of her husband and I did not like to ask. She might have been a widow. Anyway, she was a good worker and never minded what jobs she had to do – ironing sheets

21

was about my greatest bugbear at the time of the Arabs!

One morning a man selling onions came to the door. I bought a long string – and some 'garlics' and he departed.

However, on another visit some time later, he asked for my help; apparently he had lost his lodgings – his seasonal lodgings for when he brought his onions over from Brittany – and needed several months accommodation in England. He had stayed somewhere in the area but his Landlady was to retire and live with a relative in another district. I had visions of strings of onions everywhere and told him that I did not think I could entertain the idea – and also, apparently, it would not be just for him but also his teenage son, Joe.

"No, Madam," he begged. "My onions would not be here, they're in my store and we'd be no trouble and I go out early mornings doing the stringing – I would not need any breakfast, I can make myself a cup of tea if you leave the things on the kitchen table . . ." etc., etc.

Yes, Monsieur Baptiste and Joe came to stay with us. Joe was very despondent at times because his English was not good enough to let him 'haggle' with any housewife after a bargain and I believe he became depressed and disillusioned with the 'door to door' trade. Monsieur Baptiste wore 'sabot' footwear and always left them out in the porch by the front door, coming in with stocking covered feet.

True to his word Monsieur Baptiste was no trouble – as long as I looked after suppers for him and Joe. After all this time I do not quite remember how I fitted everything in but I did. My young John used to take his time over meals in those days and Monsieur would say very gravely, "Johnie will be the last one, Janet will be finished first." Usually he was right!

There was another request from the French onion man, for every time he brought his onions over he had to pay freight charges before he sold enough onions to meet the cost. This time it was a request to my husband to see if he would help – "only until I sell my onions" – and so it was, and all was settled up.

I did the washing for them both and soon found out that where he rubbed the strings of onions against his knees he was wearing his long-johns out. So I mended them for him. I think Joe must have left the stringing process to his father for there were no pairs of long-johns for him – he wore shorts most of the time!

We were treated to some jars of pickled onions and 'the garlics'.

On a subsequent visit from Brittany there was a present for me from Madame Baptiste because I had looked after them so well – a china vase showing a Breton woman in her best clothes. I value that gift.

I believe Joe joined the police force in France. He had two sisters, I know – possibly several years older than he was – but, of course, we lost touch.

Our next visitor was Uncle George – Douglas's brother. He had been working in the NAAFI somewhere abroad and came back to this country to live permanently. So for quite a time he stayed with us in Worcester Park – there are some photos of him out in the garden with the children. He was very fond of them, and I believe it was reciprocated.

Uncle George had a stammer which he tried very hard to control. I do not know how long he had suffered with this speech defect. Sometimes it was scarcely noticeable but if he was hurried or a little excited then there was a decided wait before the right words would hit the ears of any listener.

Like my husband, he had been brought up at Princetown, but I think when the time came for him to move to the second stage of his education he had gone to 'the big' school in Launceston. Was it then that he developed a stammer?

4

Uncle George

Uncle George was about ten or eleven years older than his brother Douglas.

There had been a little girl in the family, I think her name was Beatrice, 'Beatie' for short, and she would have been the link between the two brothers if unfortunate circumstances had not intervened.

Apparently she contracted bronchitis – said to be due to a walk on Dartmoor with her father when the weather 'closed in' and she caught a cold. In those days the help of the doctor was only sought as a last resort. Anyway, she died.

From what I gathered, I don't think Douglas's mother ever really got over the loss.

I must concentrate on the facts as I know them, and not return to the past.

Uncle George worked for the NAAFI during the war and continued afterwards; for several years his duties took him overseas.

As already mentioned, when he returned to England from somewhere in Africa he came and stayed with us in Worcester Park. He still worked for the NAAFI and I believe he went to Claygate; probably by train every day.

Although he tried very hard to control his stammer there were times when one felt sorry for him, and it was then that there was a temptation to finish the words for him.

His stay with us in Worcester Park was very happy but he thought he ought to look for other accommodation when he knew we were 'on the move'. He found something acceptable in a district not too far off. We never had the opportunity of visiting him there but he was always welcome to come and see us.

In time he retired and found an unfurnished flat in Mitcham. He furnished it himself and showed it off with pride when my husband and I then had the opportunity and pleasure of visiting him.

I forget just how long he lived there but he did pay us some visits to Brookside in the country, although I always had the impression that he preferred town life, and for quite a number of Christmases we took a Christmas dinner up to him there. It took some doing and planning but it was easier for us to make the journey by car than for him to come to Brookside.

He had an interest in playing bowls and we still possess a 'cup' which he won.

It was in January and February 1990, after some severe winter storms, that Uncle George became quite poorly and in April of that year (the year when Nelson Mandela came out of prison after 27 years in South Africa) Uncle George began thinking about going into a Council Home. In fact, on the 17th August 1990 he did just that and stayed for a month, after which we had to take him back to his own flat.

I do not think that he regarded it as the best rest and holiday he had had in his life – he could not wait to get home, nor the authorities to get rid of him. He did not fit in, he just did not fit in! From our weekly visits to him we could see that it was not going to work!

So he was home again. Our visits continued and we did what we could for him. On the 12th October we discovered that he was in St. Georges Hospital, Tooting. On our next visit he was in the Nelson Hospital in Wimbledon – that was on the 21st October. We visited again twice. On the 11th November he was back in his own flat.

Apparently there was no answer when someone from the council tried to make contact with him so his door was broken down.

Uncle George somehow existed for days after that, but he died on the 23rd November, my birthday.

The cremation was arranged for the 4th December 1990 – another date I remember well because Grandpa at Bremridge was buried in Sandford Churchyard on 4th December 1930.

The message on the flowers for George from his brother simply said 'Enjoy your next life' while Janet had written 'In most loving remembrance of gentle kindness'. There was a tribute from Jeyne and John; they were the only other mourners. The Reverend Elaine Thomas, a coloured lady, took the service with sympathy and compassion.

Most of the next journeys to Mitcham were undertaken by Douglas alone during the necessary clearing up operations.

When I was dusting the window-ledge one morning recently the rays of the sun alighted upon some words written – rather, printed – on a brass plate on a black marble base, and on top of this base was a metal crest within which was a little round representation of a gentleman playing bowls, in traditional manner one foot is forward on the 'mat'. The character, a man, is about to send the bowling 'ball' off on its way to the other end of the green.

Written on a 'silver' plate inlet into one of the square sides of the black marble base there is an inscription which reads 'SVBG Triples Winner 1978 G. Rowe'.

I knew there was another bowling trophy, not quite so grand perhaps but I am sure much valued by the player who received it. I found it. Probably made of bakelite or some such material, black, square-sided with a slightly higher base than the more elaborate one, and bearing the initials WBC. It was awarded to 'G. ROWE in 1966 – Finalist, Bourne Cup'.

It looks as if Uncle George was very good at the game and enjoyed it while he lived in the Wimbledon Area. I suppose it was after he had retired from working for the NAAFI in Claygate, although I do not have any dates in a diary – no, I did not keep a regular diary in those days.

Marilyn, my niece, has told me what she remembers about 'Uncle George'. One of her most outstanding memories must be when he visited her mother and father one night when they were all supposed to be going to a play put on by members of the church they attended in the district.

Uncle George tripped and fell – something to do with their front gate. Apparently it ended in him breaking his arm. Of course, all thoughts of going to any play were out of the question. The fact that I did not remember anything at all about it probably means that it happened when I was down in Devon trying to improve the Bungalow ready for the next summer visitors. Certainly it would have been before I kept a diary.

Uncle George had broken his arm when he was a schoolboy and the family lived at Princetown. He went to a school in Launceston, over the boundary of Devon and into Cornwall, maybe the most popular school for the pupils who had attained the age for moving on. I do not know whether he would have taken the appropriate exam for entry or whether it was the nearest school.

I have found my diary notes from 1990 and I will quote them as written:

2/2/90	*16/2/90 and 2/3/90:* Uncle George very poorly.
11/2/90	Nelson Mandela comes out of prison after 27 years. (S. Africa.)
6/4/90	Uncle George going into a Council Home for a rest – thinking about it.
13/4/90	Lavinia and Derek came up to dinner.
4/5/90	Uncle George very poorly.
27/7/90	do.
17/8/90	Uncle George goes to Quarterman House, London.
31/8/90	Visit to Uncle George at Quarterman House.
7/9/90	do.
14/9/90	We bring George back to his flat.
21/9/90	We visit him at home. Still poorly but happy to be home after an unfortunate 'holiday'.
28/9/90	do.
1/10/90	D.J.R. painted high windows and pipes. *[Whose?]*
5/10/90	Visit to Uncle George.
12/10/90	We discover Uncle George is in St. George's Hospital, Tooting, and visit him.
21/10/90	We visit Uncle George in Nelson Hospital, Wimbledon.
28/10/90	We visit Uncle George in Wimbledon.
9/11/90	Communication from Nelson Hospital – Uncle George going back to his own flat.
12/11/90	Doug visits Uncle George's flat as the council man is going to mend the door. (Apparently the door had to be broken when the care workers could not gain entry and they knew he should have been home.)

27

15/11/90   Doug visits the flat and met social workers.

23/11/90   Uncle George died – a happy release. Pity it was on my
birthday! He was 81 years old.

The cremation was arranged, by DJR for 4/12/90. The
Rev. Elaine Thomas, from abroad, officiated with great
kindness.

Doug's tribute was 'Enjoy your new life', and others
included 'In most loving remembrance of gentle
kindness'. Jeyne and John from Horsham were the only
other mourners. It was very cold.

Going back to the time when George was in the council
Quarterman Home with many other residents; I have rarely seen
anyone so miserable as he was. The staff were cheerful – at least
when we were there they seemed to be making an effort to please
him. Several visits had to be made to his bedroom by us as 'Mr
Rowe is resting'.

The bedroom was sparse, no ornaments worth looking at, but I
did notice a Bible on a small table or chest of drawers. I also saw
that one page had been torn out of it and I wondered if George
had done it. Without having his spectacles on he probably did not
know what he was doing, or looking at. He had his stick which,
incidentally, I now use as I had to take it when Douglas was in the
East Surrey Hospital. It is one of those black ones, with a lighter
handle and a rubber tip, and a 'broken' backbone! It did not slip
on the polished floor like the one I had to use on my first visit!

5

Auntie Audrey and Little Ronnie

To explain who these two are – or were – I have to go back to Bremridge and the farm across the valley, Prowse, and to Doddridge in the East Village area, where Grandma and Grandpa lived when they married.

Grandma seems to have been particularly fond of one of Grandpa's Sisters, Sarah, and it was a friendship which lasted all her life, extending to her daughters after their marriages to their respective husbands.

I do not know when Sarah died. She left two daughters, Maude and Nettie, and in time they married. Maude to Mr Ronnie Rathbone and Nettie to a Mr Retter. When we left Bremridge in 1930 a David Retter came down to stay with us and helped to clear up. Being only a child in those days I did not know enough about the different branches of the family really to find out who he was exactly but it could have been his son who married Nettie – I know Grandma and Mum thought quite well of him.

However, it is with Maude and her family I must continue, and I believe we were living in 84 Bath Road, Exeter, when the postman brought a letter with a London post-mark with the address written in a childish hand. Soon Grandma was in tears. "Sarah's little Granddaughter," she said, "has written to tell us that she has lost her mother, unexpectedly, after only a few days of illness – Meningitis."

Audrey had said that she would do her best to look after 'Little Ronnie' and bring him up as her mother would have done. I believe Audrey was still at school with some years to continue

29

before 'going out to work', so it was indeed quite a task for the child, and she said she would do her best to look after Daddy, too.

After we had moved to 48 Old Tiverton Road, Exeter, Audrey came down to visit us. She had a friend with her, a very nice girl called Peggy Chinn.

Audrey came to visit us in Worcester Park and I have a photo of her in a group with the relatives who were able to come to Janet's christening party but Little Ronnie is not there.

Maybe it was a throw-back to his ancestors but he became very interested in agricultural shows and the judging of animals. If he could not farm, perhaps he could judge, but anyway he went to a college somewhere and it was always interesting to talk to him about his progress.

One morning Audrey telephoned us in Worcester Park, full of tears. She scarcely knew how to tell us that Little Ronnie had had an accident and was taken to a hospital nearby and that he had died. It seems that he was at an agricultural college – I don't know where – but he and some friends went for long horse rides across the downs. One day they came out onto a hard road when he suddenly slipped from the saddle and landed on the road, sustaining concussion. She could not tell us much more than that he was taken to hospital where he died, if not immediately, then within a day or so.

Audrey said her father was heartbroken, she tried to comfort him as best she could.

I believe Audrey's first job was to work for a photographer in the district. I know they attended many weddings together when she went as his assistant helping to arrange – or rearrange – the parties concerned. She was a very attractive girl, Ronald Reitty was lucky to have such an assistant.

However, she met someone else – a Donald Cox – and eventually they were married I think or, at least, formed a partnership which yielded two children, a boy whose name I have forgotten and a little girl christened Sarah.

After we came to Brookside to live there were several telephone calls made between us but the last time I tried to telephone her there was just no line, no connection. I did wonder whether she would try to get in touch some time or other but it is now too long ago so I do not expect to hear anything more from Audrey.

I have remembered the boy's name – it came to me just as I was going upstairs to bed so I've come back to type it in immediately. The boy was called: 'Marcus' – I do not know what significance that had for Audrey, certainly unusual, perhaps Audrey and the boy's father just liked it.

'The course of true love never does run smooth' so it is said, and I know there had been problems here. In fact, I was asked if I could help. I was collected from Worcester Park by car – destination Chingford. I am not sure now what all the disagreement and bad feeling was about but I include a copy of a letter I wrote to them on the 4th October 1952 – it seems to be more of a sermon than I would have intended. At the meeting in Chingford I ended up by suggesting that we said the Lord's Prayer together, which we did – and I seemed to be the leader!

Here is a copy of the letter I sent:

> 24 The Hollands,
> Worcester Park,
> Surrey.

> 4th October 1952

My Dear Friends,

I am writing this letter to you, Audrey, my Dear, Don and Ron, for each of you to have a copy AND I hope that you will favour me by carrying your copy with you   in your pocket, in your wallet (or wherever you carry your treasures) – so that in times of difficulty you can refer to it. Perhaps you will see your way clear to act upon the advice which I will try to set down clearly – God helping me. Call it what you will – your code of behaviour, guide or just piece of plain common sense – I hope that it will afford you comfort in times of stress.

First, let me say that I feel both very humble and very proud to think that you called upon me in your crisis. I don't think that I have any power to help on my own without the strength of God behind me and for that I have prayed most earnestly. Remember, with God's help everything is possible. Leave God out and the prospect of life before one becomes bleak, to say the least of it.

Now, I feel that the next thing I should say is that I think you have a very nice little studio, shop and work-room. Everything seems to fit in so well and to be just right. It is no wonder that you

31

have done good business in the past; with a happy atmosphere and the brightness of the studio you make your 'victims' feel important, happy and comfortable and I know that you can manage to keep it that way, in spite of the work that it must mean for you all.

I am quite sure that the decisions made yesterday and born out of all the emotional stress and strain of the last few weeks mark the beginning of a new era. All of you, you must forget the past and some of the mistakes and failings which have culminated in the deadlock. I say 'some of the mistakes and failings' deliberately, because I know that we all learn from our mistakes. Those lessons learned are indeed valuable and if we are wise the same mistakes will not be repeated. I have every confidence that you will now all pull your horses together, so that you all go in the same direction. It is valuable, too, to know how to relax – as pussy on the mat did yesterday. There are bound to be some moments of difficulty ahead, but if you can remember the two little bears 'bear and forebear', I am quite sure that it will help.

Please don't ever be too hasty in judgment. If you have made a mistake about anything, or anyone, it is not climbing down to say 'I'm sorry' and really mean it. Maybe there is a sharp remark or a hasty retort on the tip of your tongue but think again, think again and think again before you let it slip out. Try to think of the effect your words may have on your listeners, and think of their feelings too.

As I have said, we have to live on from where we are, from this minute, from this hour, from this day, from this year. Try to take one thing at a time and don't worry about what *may* happen. After all, it may *never* happen.

I feel, as I am sure you all do too, that this thing which has happened is bigger than all of us. There are some occurrences which we try to fight against but which we ought to accept. The Arabs I have known seem to accept their fate with a confidence which we would do well to copy at times. 'It is the will of Allah,' they say, and they really mean it.

I am sure I have given you enough of a sermon to last you a long time and I will only say that I do most sincerely send you all my very best wishes for a very happy partnership together. If each one of you says (and means) 'It all depends on me,' I know you will succeed and will in time be able to repay the trust which we all have in you – that is 'The Wallah on the Wall', George and all of your friends.

My very last word is to remind you of one or two things which I saw yesterday during my very enjoyable journey. The van marked 'Courage'. The notice 'Jesus Christ, the same yesterday, today, and for ever'. The name of the ship 'Discovery'. Take those three things as they come. Have courage, believe in God, in Christ, in Jesus, and you will make the discovery that everything is possible with God's help.

I am sorry, there is still another thing. Just one more, and it is a very important one. Don't talk too much to your friends – any of you. In matters of the heart, with the best will in the world, words can be taken to mean what they should not really mean, and confidences can be betrayed so easily – even by a look! The harm is not intentional, but it is done. I know how one word adds to another and how very easy it is to confide in one's friends, but it is important not to. If you must tell somebody, tell God.

If things ever do take on a serious twist in the future, I beg of you, all meet together in the studio, talk things over together quietly, and say the Lord's Prayer together. Help each other always, without bias or bitterness and, again, God help you all.

Yours most sincerely,
Dorinda

Despite being a bit of a sermon, I do hope this was of some help for the couple.

Although not connected, thinking of these people from the past has reminded me that there are 'Reeds' on my side of the family and also on my husband's. Our Reed goes back to Mary Ann Stoyle, Grandpa's sister, who seems to have left Devon; certainly Uncle Reed and Auntie Nellie lived in London. It was their visit every summer that Lavinia and I thought was a 'highlight' – Uncle was interested in looking round out of doors, walking over some of the grass fields of Bremridge and admiring the views. I remember that he spoke very well – 'posh' we called it.

Auntie Nellie would be indoors talking to Grandma in the sitting-room – always a lunch (dinner to us) had been provided and Mum and whoever was helping in the kitchen were busy with the chores. There was always a tea-time and it was then that the black teapot came into its own. There was custard, cream and apple pie, sometimes with the addition of gooseberries or raspberries. I never remember having strawberries at Bremridge, but there were plenty of blackberries – quite often picked by Lavinia and me the day before.

Then it was time for them to return to Prowse and the pony and trap were made ready – the pony would have been stabled all day, probably with a bit of hay available, and that would be their visit over for another year.

Of course, there were letters to Grandma; she did not relate any of Auntie's news to us children. Now and again there would be a parcel from London and Mum turned garments to good account for Lavinia and me.

6

A Very Near Thing

The post was usually delivered in Worcester Park after Douglas had left for his office job in London.

One morning an 'official' looking envelope arrived and by that time he was probably already in his office so the letter sat in the usual collecting place until he came home, but I did wonder what it meant. A letter from the War Office!

At that time there was trouble about the Suez Canal. Speaking from memory I believe that Anthony Eden was one of the parliamentarians mainly involved in whatever trouble was brewing. He did become 'Sir', probably later.

In those days whatever important letter arrived people did not immediately reach for the telephone and communicate: good news or bad – it had to wait until the intended recipient came home again, so this envelope waited.

In due course Douglas arrived home and, even now, after all these years, the sight of his face as he read the letter is something which I cannot forget.

Yes, it was from the War Office, instructing him to present himself duly for medical examination – date was given, of course.

He had no choice – or at least I do not think he had – so on the due date he presented himself at the address given.

Recounting his experience afterwards he said that the doctors were very thorough – much more exact that time than when he had been called up for National Service at the beginning of the 1939 war. Then it had been a case of, "Are you all right, lad, got all the right equipment and can you see straight? Sign on!"

This time it was quite different. I gathered that there were several examiners, each careful, and then they came to the last one. This doctor studied his hands finger by finger, and he did not seem satisfied, and so Douglas was rejected.

It was possibly an accident of birth but Douglas's little finger on one hand was slightly bent – he never could put it straight out. As he was in the Signals apparently he would, or could, have been involved in passing important messages and, maybe, doctor thought that bend in the little finger was important enough for rejection.

Actually, in wartime Douglas said that he often had to pass on very important messages indeed and often 'high-ups' were involved. A bent little finger did not matter then!

The following chapter is written by Douglas in answer to a question from his grandson Danny about his wartime experiences.

7

The 1930s and Douglas's Wartime Experiences
written by Douglas

Pay and prices were very low compared to today. For instance, I started my first job in 1934 with Plymouth City Council with a salary of £75 a *year*. In 1935 I moved on to Post Office Telephones for a salary of £90 per *year*. In 1936 I bought my first bicycle – a new Rudge – costing £5. I could not afford to pay it all at once, and had to pay by instalments over twelve months.

There was a firm called 'Fifty Shilling Tailors'. The name tells you how much a suit could cost! (£2.50 in today's money.)

One cannot omit mention of the war. While we in Britain were gradually improving our way of life, Hitler and his Nazis were gaining power in Germany. In 1935 Germany reoccupied the Rhineland, and later invaded Austria and Czechoslovakia before attacking Poland in 1939. This caused Britain and France to declare war on Germany in September in order to try to stop them before they started on us. The war put an end to most people's hopes and prospects. Many people in the British Isles were killed, many ships sunk by torpedoes, depth charges and U-boats. The Germans bombed some of our cities and we bombed theirs, but most of the fighting took place just after the 1930s, although war was actually declared on a Sunday morning early in September 1939.

I am grateful to Danny for his enquiry as to what I did during the Second World War, and will give a brief résumé of some of the happenings.

Strictly speaking, I was in the First World War as I was born before it ended in 1918!

My war service really started in September 1938 – a year before war was declared.

In September 1935, I joined the Post Office Telephone Service after passing a Civil Service exam, plus a medical examination and character references. I worked at the Telephone Manager's Office in Exeter, which was responsible for the South West: Cornwall, Devon, Somerset and Dorset.

In September 1938, after Hitler had invaded Czechoslovakia (he had already occupied the Rhineland and annexed Austria) our Government had to admit that it was necessary to start building up our defences (Winston Churchill had been telling them this for years). They therefore authorised the building of new Army camps, military hospitals, RAF stations, emergency headquarters for police, fire, and ambulance, and air-raid precautions including shelters, the Observer Corps and various other organisations.

Each of these projects needed telephone facilities, and requests started flooding in to the Telephone Manager's Office. I was then taken off normal civilian work and given special duty dealing with defence orders. This kept me busy until the end of 1939.

Through contact with the Area Signal Officer, through whom the military orders came, I was invited to join his unit when the time came for me to enlist. It seemed a good idea, so in December 1939, I joined the Royal Signals.

The job of this corps was to provide telephone, teleprinter, radio services and despatch riders for other Army corps and units, and instruction as necessary.

It also provided telephone and teleprinter services for RAF groups and units.

I worked at the Area Headquarters for some months, and then had a chance to learn to operate telephone switchboards. This involved a move to an old Napoleonic fort on a headland overlooking Plymouth Sound – part of a ring of forts surrounding Plymouth. The switchboard was manned by one operator at a time but as it had to be manned 24 hours a day there were three operators doing shift work. There were also technicians to maintain the equipment, lines and cables. Most of the fort was occupied by part of an infantry regiment. It was very pleasant there on the headland apart from one occasion when German bombers dropped a shower of incendiary bombs on the fort as part of an air-raid on the city. I was outdoors at the time and managed to shelter under a rampart while they fell. I was then able to dodge around the burning incendiaries to a safer place.

After a few months there I was posted to an Army camp with a very busy switchboard north of Plymouth. This was a very useful experience, but early in 1941 I was summoned to work in the office of the Chief Signal Officer, Southern Command, near Salisbury, Wiltshire.

While there I had to go on a couple of training courses. One involved firing a rifle on a rifle range, throwing live grenades, and an assault course. The other was about using a Bren machine-gun and a Sten gun, taking them to pieces, cleaning and putting them together again.

There was also some bayonet practice on a dummy; a sack stuffed with sawdust, old papers, etc. I made sure that dummy would not attack me again!

For the last year I was there we had to do a three or four mile cross-country run once a week to keep fit. Quite enjoyable!

In September 1943, I was posted to an Air Formation Signals in Yorkshire. This type of unit would provide telephone and teleprinter services for RAF groups and their subsidiary unit. All the forces were building up for D-day, but we did not then have an Air Formation to look after!

As I had suffered a hernia I was sent to Catterick Hospital to have it repaired, then to Darlington as 'walking wounded', Barnard Castle for remedial exercises and then to a military depot for toughening up; gymnasium work, a route march, cross-country runs and an assault course. Then back to my unit at Huddersfield, where I was given a job in the Quartermaster Stores.

In May 1944, we moved South to the London area to be ready for D-day. My section was living in tents at an RAF Group HQ, West of London, and for weeks had been loading our trucks with various equipment.

When D-day dawned we were told that another section had been sent first, and we were to go later.

The section which did go suffered a direct hit on the beaches; men were killed and injured and equipment destroyed.

My section did not go till August, from Southampton to

Normandy. When we were about half way there our landing craft sprang a leak. Fortunately, the crew got the pumps going and we were able to keep going; the craft was run straight on to the beach when we got there. It was near Greye-sur-mer – a little village near Caen. The rest of the convoy had to wait their turn to use the Mulberry harbour.

Because the craft had to beach we were several miles away from where we were supposed to be and had to find our way along the coast to find the transport which was to take us to our camp. This was about five miles inland in a large orchard.

Our first job was to erect a number of six-man tents under the apple trees (which provided useful cover) and camp beds ready for the night. Then a meal and finding our way around.

Next day we started work – manning a large switchboard (and teleprinter room) for an RAF Group HQ located in a chateau near the coast. As usual we had various shifts covering 24 hours a day.

During our trips to and from the camp we used to see country women washing clothes in a stream which ran by their cottages, and rubbing them on flat slabs of stone nearby.

There were a number of burnt-out tanks, etc., in the area and relics of the fighting two months or so earlier. One had to be careful – there were mines in the verge outside our camp.

Adjoining the camp was a cottage where the owner (or tenants) lived. A cow was tethered not far from the house, and twice a day the old lady would come out with a bucket and stool, sit down and milk the cow.

By September the evening mists became very chilly and penetrating. Some nights I turned in fully dressed, with blankets and great coat on top to keep warm.

The country was not very attractive, and I quite understood why William the Conqueror decided to come to England in 1066! In fact, according to a genealogical history, one of my ancestors came with him.

I was able to visit Bayeux Cathedral and see the ancient tapestry depicting the Norman invasion. No doubt it had been well hidden during the German occupation.

It was at the camp that I had my narrowest escape. I and half a dozen other chaps had the task of transferring petrol from a dump of 40-gallon drums to 4-gallon jerrycans ready for our forthcoming move to Belgium – to be carried as a reserve supply on our vehicles.

Our 'equipment' was primitive – one hand-operated rotary pump. We tied the pump to an apple tree, manhandled a drum (weighing about 3½ cwt) over to the pump, put the suction hose in the drum and the outlet hose in the jerrycan, and started pumping. The system worked.

Then a young chap who was off duty came along to see what we were doing. No objection to that – until we saw that he had a cigarette between his lips and was cupping a cigarette lighter in his hands to light it! He was shouted at – hard! We just managed to stop him; in another second he would have lit it and we should all have gone up in a fireball. Petrol was pouring out of the drums and into the cans, some had been spilt, and the air was thick with petrol vapour. There were between 1,000 and 1,500 gallons in the dump. Our young 'friend' did not stay long after that – he did not feel welcome. He was generally in a dream when off duty, but he nearly took his dreams too far that time.

We carried on with the job until we had enough for our vehicles.

At the end of September we moved on to Brussels where I and two other men had to man a switchboard serving an RAF transport unit. We were located in the basement – a favourite place for telephone equipment, safer in case of bombing, etc., and easier for the engineers.

One undesirable feature, however, was that when there was heavy rain the sewers would flood up into the basement!

There was a large furnace which provided hot water for the whole building, and we took it upon ourselves to act as stokers.

Brussels was an attractive city, and I was sorry to leave when after a month or so we had to move to Antwerp, in the Flemish part of Belgium.

Antwerp was, and is, one of the biggest ports in Europe, and was the main port for bringing in supplies for our Army and RAF. We had to provide telephone and teleprinter services for an RAF equipment unit which was busily engaged on that work.

The enemy was well aware of the importance of the port to us and decided to try to put it out of action.

Thus, a few days after we arrived there the Germans started to bombard the fort and town with V1s and V2s.

The V1 was a flying bomb, powered by a noisy engine. It was

set on course for its target, with a measured fuel supply; when the fuel was used up the V1 dived to the ground and its one ton of explosive detonated. It was also known as a 'doodle bug'.

The V2 was a rocket propelled bomb – also carrying a one-ton warhead. It would be known as a ballistic missile now. There was no warning as to where and when it would land.

The noisy engine of the V1 was an advantage, as it would wake me up as it approached at night. When I heard the engine cut out I would pull the blankets up over my head so that when the blast shattered the windows no harm was done. After that, turn back the blankets and go to sleep again!

Eventually all the glass was broken, and the windows boarded up.

One afternoon when off duty, I was in the town centre and stopped at a cinema. It was showing a Wild West film. I stayed several minutes looking at the photographs, etc., but decided not to go in, and walked on. A few minutes later it had a direct hit by a V2, which reduced it to a heap of rubble with about 600 bodies underneath.

The Antwerp City Council records show that during the six months I was there about 2,500 V1s and 2,500 V2s fell on the city. Everybody had a number of near misses, of course, but they did not stop the port from functioning.

In May 1945, Germany surrendered.

The war was not finished, however, and we still had to soldier on.

After a couple of weeks break near Brussels I was moved to a different set-up at Mons. I worked in the Belgian barracks there (which our Forces had occupied). I was still in the Royal Signals but attached to the 14th Somerset Yeomanry for administrative purposes, and I went to a nearby American Army canteen for meals. There were also some German prisoners whom I had to help guard at one time.

Mons was the scene of very heavy fighting in the First World War. During one of my off-duty walks I came across a First World War Cemetery. The crosses marking the graves stretched in straight rows radiating in every direction as far as one could see. The ages of those who died were shown – mostly 18, 19, or the early twenties. Very impressive and very sad.

I was not allowed to stay there long – it was on to Germany.

We went through the devastated Ruhr Industrial Area, stayed a night at Bonn – then just a village by the River Rhine – and next day through some beautifully wooded country to Bad Oeynhausen in Westphalia, which had been taken over for the Headquarters of the British Army of the Rhine, (BAOR).

The town's telephone exchange had also been taken over, and I spent some time there. The switchboard occupied three sides of a large room and had positions for about fifty operators.

Conditions were changing, however, and the exchange was being used more for rehabilitation purposes; there was so much to be done to rebuild German industries, re-house the homeless and feed them. Civilian operators with international exchange experience, and preferably more than one language, were being brought in to replace military personnel, so I was not sorry to move to the rear headquarters where conditions were more congenial, at Herford.

Bad Oeynhausen is, as the name Bad indicates, a spa town with very ornate baths supplied by the medicinal spring waters. I was able to sample the luxury of a large bath there once.

At Herford I was billeted in a bungalow; the family had left. There was a garden, and a pigsty built on to the rear wall of the house at basement level, with a door opening into the basement so that the pigs could be let into the basement during severe weather. It seemed a very practical arrangement, but I think there must have been a certain amount of 'pig pong' wafting its way up the stairs to the living rooms.

Once, while exploring the countryside, I came across a group of about a hundred Germans chopping wood to take home (there was no coal available that winter).

It occurred to me that if they chose to be awkward I should be at a disadvantage! However, there was only one thing to do – I walked straight through the middle of the group. They stopped work, we looked at each other, and I walked on. Not a word was said. (I did not speak German and I do not suppose any of them knew English.)

Later I had a lift along the autobahn, back to base, in one of the earliest Volkswagon cars to be built.

Eventually it was time for me to be demobilised – I was more than ready to go after six years in the Army. A truck to the station, a slow journey by train to Calais and on the way the train had to cross a wide river on a temporary bridge made of timber where speed was restricted to about two miles per hour. It was a relief to get to the other side!

At Calais, if the weather permitted, a steamer would cross the Channel. It was a smooth trip, unlike the previous one when I had leave for a few days as then the ferry and the escorting destroyer were zig-zagging across the Channel in case of U-boat attack.

I arrived at Folkestone Barracks, exchanged my uniform for a civilian suit, and went home for a leave of three months.

Then back to work with the Post Office Telephones. It was hard at first to have to work in an office all day after the varied life I had been living. Still, I had to be thankful that I had a job and home to come back to, many others did not.

Well, that is enough for now. It is all true. I did not have to do anything heroic (thank goodness), but I did my best, and my duty, as millions of others did.

PS: I nearly got caught for the Korean War. In 1951 I had a letter from the Royal Signals Record Office saying that I was to be recalled to the Army (I was still on the Army Reserve).

But first I had to have a medical examination by about six doctors. Everything seemed OK until I reached the last doctor. He was very interested in my hands, especially certain fingers. He looked at his little book of instructions, then examined the fingers and wrote his report.

A few weeks later I was told that I would not now be recalled as I was medically unfit. I wondered why as I felt OK.

I remembered later that during the war the grades of Switchboard Operator and Teleprinter Operator had been amalgamated. That meant that anybody joining the grade in future would need to be able to do high speed typing for teleprinter work, as well as operating switchboards.

But three of my fingers have slight irregularities which prevent me from doing high speed typing! That is why I was 'unfit'!

I was very grateful to those fingers!

8

School Days

As soon as we arrived in Worcester Park we had to see about a school for Jeyne and she started at the Malden Parochial School which was the nearest, 'up the road and along the top' – possibly about half a mile off, certainly well within walking distance.

Mr Harman was the headmaster, Mrs Broome his 'second-in-command' – I did not have the pleasure of meeting either of them as Douglas went with Jeyne on her first day and eventually little brother John followed on.

I think the school had quite a good reputation for getting the children through the eleven-plus but I was more than a little disappointed when I heard that they did not think that Jeyne would get through.

Very recently I found the School Reports put away in a drawer. On the last one for Jeyne there was the remark that she was able but did not always speak up!

I had always encouraged her to read. Even in Exeter I can remember walking up Old Tiverton Road with John in his pram and Jeyne pausing to read the letters off the road sign erected by contractors doing some repairs to a public service – water mains or telephone. The men were quite amused and I can remember saying, "Thank you for the use of your blackboard."

There were other mothers in 'The Hollands' with girls of the same age – all hoping their daughters would pass the dreaded exam so I took action to help them and Jeyne, of course.

I think I obtained exam material, and every afternoon after school they joined Jeyne's little class in my sitting-room and we worked through everything together – even young Janet had her little pencil and book which soon became full of squiggles no one could read.

We waited anxiously for the exam results and when they were announced all three of 'my students' had passed, so I can tell you there was great rejoicing in 'The Hollands'!

9

Thinking of Finding a New Home

I believe that my husband had a change of departments in London in the Civil Service, he had something to do with the Ministry of Supply at one time and I am right, I think, in saying that he was dealing with and checking animal skins which came in from abroad. Then I am sure The Board of Trade came into it somewhere, and that could have included 'the skin trade'.

It was certain that the daily journey to London would continue for a very long time and, again, the trains were becoming so full that 'standing room only' seemed to have become the order of the morning and evening travel.

Jeyne had passed 'The Common Entrance', but it was not only on her education that our decision was taken – young Janet was now due to start somewhere, so if we were going everything pointed to this being about the right time.

Of course we studied the local papers and the most attractive areas seemed to us to be Redhill or Reigate. We made several journeys and did actually look at about four properties – I remember one was on a hill in Redhill – a very steep hill – the decoration being a very deep and depressing green! So that was ruled out.

We advertised our Worcester Park home and I felt really sorry to be leaving it but time passes, things move on, and almost immediately there was a buyer.

One of the papers we studied carried an advertisement for a buyer of a smallholding with approximately ten acres. We contacted the owner, or owners, Mr and Mrs Charlesworth, and to

47

cut a long story short they were going to Canada to live. Their property was in the Nutfield area and it sounded interesting.

Before going any further we took a day off and went to Nutfield Station to look around and see what the village had to offer. There was also a cottage near a cross-road junction for sale; very nice, large garden, thatched roof, three bedrooms, etc., but it did not really appeal to us. For one thing it was very near to a road junction and we thought it could be a bit of a risk for young children.

Another day we went to Redhill and had a bus ride 'along the top', getting out beside a school, crossing the road and walking a little way down the hill towards South Nutfield Village. What a view, we could see for miles all down to the south and I believe we picked out Gatwick Racecourse. We thought we must be lucky if the property down in the valley really did become ours!

Me – Dorinda.

My husband Douglas.

Douglas and me together.

The Bungalow at Heath Bridge – showing Bremridge Farm
buildings above on the right.

The Bungalow at Heath Bridge.

Back view of The Hollands, Worcester Park.

Uncle George with Jeyne and John at Worcester Park.

Douglas nursing 'Potchy Cot' at Exeter.

Douglas second from left in back row, with a group
taking a break from wartime duties.

10

Leaving Worcester Park

In many ways I felt a little sorry to be leaving Worcester Park. After all, we were comparatively near to the railway station and to a shopping centre, and the near neighbours had become friends. Kingston with all its big shops was only a bus ride away, as also was Sutton, although we had not visited either centre very often.

Yes, the neighbours had been very friendly, Mrs Hunt next door 'down' kept up correspondence with me for several years. I have never seen apple trees trimmed like the ones in their garden, they did bear fruit but seemed to be more or less skeletons and not at all like normal trees – our fully-leafed specimen in my young days at Bremridge would have turned up their noses in disgust, if that was possible!

The family on the other side of us was equally friendly. Again, there were three children – a 'big boy' who had nearly finished his schooling, a 'middle boy' who is now an MP (Labour Party, I believe) somewhere up north. I would not have recognised him as the slim child I knew because he has put on much weight. The youngest was a girl several years older than Jeyne. I did not know of this at the time but Jeyne has told me since that she was afraid the older girl was going to carry out her threat of taking away Jeyne's doll's pram and generally teasing her. Children can be very unkind, or perhaps unthinking could best describe their behaviour.

Further up the road two sisters lived together – the Misses Dench. One of them was only too glad to come and spend an

49

evening with us and she was only too happy to be able to do a little sewing, perhaps mend the socks – and I believe they wore out much more quickly in those days since not so much nylon seemed to be used in their production. I know this Miss Dench had great difficulty in sleeping at night.

Opposite us there was quite a plump lady with a dainty little daughter – like a little fairy with her fair curly hair and blue eyes. She was a pleasant little girl.

Down the other side of 'The Hollands' there were the 'copper -tops', fair skinned and freckled. The little girl here had been one of the pupils I helped to get through the eleven-plus and her mother was so pleased that she brought over a bottle of home-made wine to celebrate. We did, and I am afraid if affected me to the extent that I sat down and laughed and laughed – and I did not know what I was laughing at. I suppose it was because I was not used to 'drinking' but it did not affect her at all!

Another neighbour grew wonderful flowers – until the frost came! But I must move on for we are leaving Worcester Park behind.

11

Brookside Cottage

I believe we were met at the station (South Nutfield, of course) by Mr Charlesworth, the vendor. I think it was about lunch-time when we arrived at the white cottage.

The entrance gate was right out beside the lane, I noticed that it dragged a bit when it was shut behind us. It had obviously seen better days but was still a wide wooden barrier, a gate.

We were welcomed by Mrs Charlesworth and provided with a cup of tea in the other room while the diners finished their meal; speaking from memory I think there were about three people.

Well, we looked around. The back door was like a stable door, cut right across the middle. The kitchen had red tiles on the floor on which stood a tall kitchen dresser. The other three downstairs rooms all had 'solid' floors – and still have! Underneath the large draining board the space was filled by shelves on which cooking equipment was stored.

We looked round outside, at the size of two lawns, the squarish one at the back while the other one bordered two sides of the building and this bore a date, 1862, so there was no question as to its age. Then, though, Brookside had been two cottages which were occupied by two families of farm labourers. I have heard since that seven or eight children lived in the 'far' part. How did they all manage?

Yes, there was an indoor toilet which I believe had been adapted from the scullery of the 'far' part by the Charlesworths. The old toilets at the side of each cottage were empty except for the storage of logs or coal, feeding the Rayburn with the fuel it

51

needed. Again, I think the Charlesworths had installed it for it looked 'newish'.

Electricity came from the mains but water was another matter. It was a piped supply which came from the Redhill Aerodrome over the first lawn, and bills came from them. They also supplied the water for the two cottages inside the aerodrome perimeter which had been airmen's billets in wartime, and I believe two further cottages up the hill towards Outwood also depended on Redhill Aerodrome for their supply.

Not far from the back door there is a depression in the lawn which had obviously been a well at some time – I do not know if both the original cottages had to use it; if so it must have been very hard work dipping and carrying, especially for the far dwelling!

The Charlesworths intended going to Canada as soon as the sale was through and would be leaving several items of furniture behind, so what did we think of Brookside? Mr Charlesworth drove us back to Redhill Station across the aerodrome.

We had learned that part of the land belonging to Brookside was being used by a college for the instruction of the pupils in agricultural pursuits. If we seriously thought of buying the property it was hoped that this arrangement could continue.

There was not too much time for prolonged deliberations as the Charlesworths were anxious to begin their new life in Canada. As far as we were concerned it certainly seemed that if we were going to leave Worcester Park now was the time to do it – with Jeyne to begin at a new school, John to continue his education somewhere and Janet still to start hers.

So Brookside Cottage became ours in 1955, complete with the furniture which the previous owners were anxious to leave behind, and their large yellow dog, George – and thereby hangs a tale of sorrow for he was killed by the Jersey Milk Lorry the very next morning after our move. He had run across the lane after a rabbit or cat, or something.

Our own furniture could not come for two or three days, but we were able to ask Mr and Mrs Charlesworth to come down to tea before they left their friends up at the corner of Crab Hill Lane, where they were staying for at least a few days. I forget just what we had but I know they were very impressed. They said they thought we would make a success of the holding.

The first poultry house still exists but now, in 2002, it is more than a little shabby and every time we are subject to extreme wind or a storm I begin to wonder what damage will be suffered there. In those days it held about fifty fowls, I refuse to say 'chicken' because to me and all my early memories from the Bremridge days that term only refers to young birds and certainly not those of an age to lay eggs.

The birds which we had inherited were old – or oldish – and certainly did not produce many eggs. We considered they would soon have to be replaced and that is why I went to a farm sale in the Edenbridge district, bid for and bought pullets, another small house and several oddments, feeders, etc. It was from this sale that the purchases were delivered by a one-eyed coalman with a gammy leg!

We were not popular with the children, and all because we sent them to school for the three weeks of the term which remained. Douglas went with Jeyne and John, while I accompanied Janet to the local Junior School. I think it took the children a long time to forgive us for not letting them stay at home until the summer holidays started.

The arrangement with the college to use part of the land for demonstration purposes for the pupils continued for several years, but it did eventually come to an end, although I have forgotten the circumstances leading to this.

So far, I have not mentioned the young man we 'took over' when we came to Brookside. He lived in a very small caravan stationed in the bottom of the field not too far from the Brook – in fact, in times of flooding I believe he had to 'make himself scarce'.

Mrs Charlesworth had been providing him with meals, particularly dinners if he was around for the mid-day meal, and of course, I did the same.

This young man was a great pigeon fancier – he was very enthusiastic over his racers, and I believe the care of his beloved feathered friends was his main reason for living in that isolated position. From time to time his favourites were put in the basket and taken to the place of release, wherever that may have been. Then he talked of awaiting the return of his birds. There were times when they did come home in good time, but would sit on the roof of his loft and not allow themselves to get caught so that

53

the ring and time of return could be registered.

Fred seemed to know how to do everything connected with agriculture and country pursuits and with his help and encouragement we tilled part of the ground to a cereal crop. In time it was ready to cut and harvest, arranged again through this young man, and successfully completed.

After the harvest, to be able to use the grain for feeding to poultry, the crop has to be thrashed, and that needed 'the drasher' as we used to say in Devon. So, in through the bottom gateway on Crab Hill Lane came the 'thresher' on to our field.

The children were very excited and keen to watch the monster churning out the grain from the chaff, and to me it was as if I had stepped back in time to the visit of the thresher in the court at Bremridge. There it had been much more of an occasion and something to be aware of if you were on the way to or from school and were unfortunate to meet it in the narrow road from East Village or, worse still, going up Bremridge Lane. I can remember once going behind the gorse bushes to avoid 'the creature' puffing steam or smoke. The hill was steep and I did not know anything about controls or brakes.

Over several years we had increased our number of poultry houses from one to five and had added a house where pigs could be reared. The trade in eggs was good and as long as you were happy and pleasant when customers came, no matter what the work position was indoors, and you had time for them, then they nearly always came back. I had several customers who came at weekends from London and I was always very pleased to see them.

We also had a pigs' house where weaners were looked after. Invariably customers with small children would 'invite trouble' by taking a young child up in their arms high enough to look over the wall to see 'the little choogies' and the little choogies would either run to the corner of the house away or become inquisitive and grunt up at the viewers, sometimes causing a howl of fright!

The little Sales Shed was really a small poultry house, actually the one bought at the sale I attended at Edenbridge and brought to Brookside with other poultry equipment by the coalman with a gammy leg! We soon found out that there was life in the shed apart from us, and before we could use it the creepy-crawlies had to be expelled. So there was a great disinfectant and drying out period. It was provided with a long 'counter' down one side – this had been the base of Mrs Charlesworth's draining board. A small chest of drawers on the other side of the little shed usually held the egg measuring or weighing equipment, while empty trays or boxes were at the back of the shed, so no space was wasted.

We bought day old chicks of the kind which should lay eggs, and eggs, and eggs! That is unless something untoward happened to them in the growing stages – it seemed as if, at times, they were hell bent on killing themselves – such as when they started feather pecking and eating each other from the tail end upwards!

When Mr Williams, our 'Food Man', called – yes, another 'Mr Williams' and I will tell you a little about him later – I told him what was happening and asked for his advice. Were we feeding them all right? The house was a traditional poultry house, plenty of light and ventilation.

He looked all round and watched the birds for a few minutes and then he said, "Your trouble is the sun, coming in and showing up any dust on the tail feathers – make it nearly dark in here or you will have more trouble."

We cloaked up the windows so that very little light penetrated. It seemed to work for there were no more chickens with 'cherry ends' which had been pecked raw before they died! Members of the poultry tribe can be very cruel to each other.

This Mr Williams was Brian, Bryn for short, although I never used his Christian name. He was a very cheerful character, always seemed full of fun though there was a great sadness in his life. He had a twin brother and they were very close to each other, and they went in the Army together where his twin was killed right beside him! I think he did his best to get over it by being almost 'too cheerful'.

12

School Days from Brookside

As already mentioned, I do not think we were ever forgiven by the children for sending them to school for the month or so of the term which remained before the long summer holidays, but go to school they did. Jeyne and John to the Top Nutfield School and Janet to Trindles Road in the Village.

Jeyne and John certainly had a long walk all the way up to the top of the hill – the hill from which we first looked over the valley and admired both the near and the distant views. They were tired when they reached home in the afternoons.

Janet would go with me on my bicycle. How did I have a lady's bicycle in those days for I certainly did not have one in Worcester Park? However, I was able to use somebody's 'boneshaker' to give her a lift until we came to the hill leading into South Nutfield, she had to walk up and ride down again to the corner along Mid Street up under the Railway Bridge and, eventually, into Trindles Road.

I used to meet her again when she came out of school where several of us mothers were waiting to collect our offspring.

Jeyne only had those few weeks at Top Nutfield School for after August she went to Reigate County School for Girls by train every day.

John continued his early education at Nutfield. One of his arithmetic books bore the headmaster's remark, 'Well done, Mum', I remember! He had several years there but just missed success in the Common Entrance Exam, by only a few marks I believe, and so continued his education at Bletchingly. I must have been over there once or twice but I never really knew the headmaster. John rarely spoke about 'Sir'.

In due course Janet also took that dreaded exam. She passed but I don't think both girls were at Reigate County School at the same time. As with youngsters today 'school' was regarded as an unavoidable necessity where as well as the lessons your height and sight were checked and sometimes visits to the dentist were arranged. The clinic serving this school area was over at Shaws Comer in Reigate and I remember my train journeys over there to accompany one or other somewhat reluctant child. Fortunately nothing terrible was ever discovered to be wrong although, of course, each one faced the prospect of medical examination with some trepidation.

13

Flying the Coop

The young man who lived in the caravan at the bottom of the field was still at Brookside when the youngsters left school and Jeyne sometimes accompanied him on his turfing jobs. I believe one of them was at the top of the aerodrome near the next lane.

She also had a filling-in job cycling down to an elderly couple in Smallfield and looking after their chickens. The term 'chickens' seems to cover anything from day-old chicks to old hens nowadays. There was a very small payment but I think she liked the elderly couple and maybe, too, the ride every morning.

After a while she decided to get a job in Redhill, another short term gap year until she really decided what she would like to do, what she would find interesting and fulfilling. So she answered an advertisement to be given training as a shorthand typist with the Coal Board in London.

She stayed there for several years, often doing work in her notebook for Lord Robens; she enjoyed that job very much and made some good friends.

When she needed to change she went to Gatwick, still as a shorthand typist.

I do not know which came first, her job there or the holiday she arranged for herself in America. I believe she was away for three whole weeks, not remaining in one place but travelling by 'Greyhound' coaches. I know she met members of a family over there with whom she corresponded for years – probably still does.

Another trip she organised for herself was around the southern part of Ireland, nearly running out of somewhere to stay one night until she found a convent where she could be smuggled into the kitchen and given a comfortable chair to rest in. I think she was on her own in Ireland but she had one or two girl friends of like mind to herself who liked travelling and youth hosteling. It was on one such trip that she spent some hours with an old lady who was making jam – "You keep stirring it, dear, and I'll make you a cup of tea." I must say that we, as parents, were not too happy about these trips into the unknown but did not like to stand in her way too much and, of course, it was on a 'hike' that she discovered where my father lived with Nancy, his housekeeper then but she did become his wife.

14

Establishing a Dairy Herd

When John left school at Bletchingly he took a job with a family across the aerodrome who kept pigs. So, in time and with Fred's help, a pigsty was put up bordering the path down to the fowl-houses. It was the inhabitants of this house who used to poke their noses up over the wall to look at the children who were so interested in them. I wonder what the pigs' reactions could have been to the squirming little red-faced 'creatures' being held securely above the wall!

Then the caravan dweller had a friend who worked in a local slaughter house, and one day such a good calf was brought in that somebody suggested that it should be found a home. You know where it ended up, yes, at Brookside, and to accommodate it a breeze-block house of ample proportions was constructed up by the oak trees.

Of course all the regulations would have to be observed, and they were. The first was the test stipulated by the Ministry of Agriculture as it was then, now DEFRA. A lady vet came to carry out the test and Josie had been tethered on a chain not far from her house.

"Oh dear," said Lady Vet, "I don't like to see a calf tethered." We soon found out why – calf and chain had Lady Vet on the ground in the twinkling of an eye, and all my offspring could do was to laugh. However, they did help and the test was carried out. The results were satisfactory, and the little heifer lived to tell the tale!

In time, in due time, with the aid of Artificial Insemination she produced a calf, and we stopped the daily deliveries from the milkman. Our friend in the caravan did the milking – lovely fresh milk but no good for the figure. We managed to scald some milk and made Devonshire cream – I can tell you that was a treat indeed!

As already mentioned, the food firm representative at that time was a Mr Williams. Mr Williams knew of some good Jersey heifer calves for sale, privately if possible but otherwise they would go to market. It is odd how everything fits into place; we had a lorry body parked in the run part of the field and this is where the Jersey heifers lodged until they grew too big for that accommodation and were off milk substitute.

Soon after we took over all the field from the college boys we grew some corn – don't ask me whether it was wheat, barley or oats – I don't remember – but I have already said what a treat it was to have the thresher on our land down by the gate on the road towards the bridge. I am sure that our caravan dweller helped and I believe he enjoyed it almost as much as I did; although my job was to supply cups of tea and home-made cakes. I had prepared them in advance.

The shed up by the garage had already been extended and it was here that it was convenient to store the grain. That shed became a dry sheltered haven for all the rough wood picked up around the hedges where they were left in the traditional way and not pared down to about half their height. It also sheltered the modern sheets of plastic and other roofing material which had accumulated from purchases made when 'sellers' or dealers came from other areas with 'bargains'. One came about every two years – an elderly gentleman who had been quite ill, and his bargains usually turned out to be very useful.

Being so near to the Redhill Aerodrome, a large expanse of nothingness except grass, there is little to break the force of the wind from that direction and sometimes we have been made only too well aware of it when part of the roof of some shed has been damaged if not completely removed! It is then that the pieces of plastic, corrugated or plain, come into their own.

When John was old enough to learn to drive a car he had lessons some evenings from the local policeman – a very nice young gentleman who lived in Top Nutfield, I believe there was an established Police House up there in those days. Often I was invited to sit in the back of our vehicle and keep quiet and observe as much of the countryside as I could. John took the test, accompanied by someone from our village. He passed first time.

Douglas's method of transport had changed since we came to Brookside. First he cycled to Nutfield Station and took the train to London – I do not know his destination there but think he was just about able to walk to his office across London Bridge. Then he bought a scooter and swooped out around the gate before scorching off up the hill, not to Nutfield Station but to Coulsdon where he could get a seat, at least for a while.

Then came a little three-wheeler which did at least give him protection from the weather, and last of all there was a Ford car. There is still a Ford car up in the garage beside the shed, disused now for several years, but it could have been a possibility for one of the younger generation.

As our herd size had increased and grown from young stock into heifers we had to think of getting them 'stocked' in other words put into calf. To do this in those days there was always a young man – not the same one – who came from the AI Centre and did what was necessary. Believe me, we were flabbergasted when a girl arrived and donned the gear (a heavy waterproof apron) and a pair of wellington boots. She was competent and took all the details when she returned to the house.

We had not just remained with our ten acres only, but had rented other land nearby and there came a time when we had to consider our milking ability. So we advertised for a milking bail and received a letter from someone at Odiham who wrote that he had one for sale which had been on Salisbury Plain where he had milked the cows on iron wheels for years! Needless to say it had been shifted to a farm near to where he now lived.

I remember that John and I went over to Odiham to see him and spent some time talking about farming and the old days. He must have trusted me because I could not meet his asking price in full just then but promised to send it on as soon as it was available. So we bought the milking bail, and I kept my part of the bargain.

Our last hurdle was to satisfy the Ministry of Agriculture and the Milk Marketing Board of our competence to produce good clean milk and that we had adequate facilities for everything – provision of water, hay store, food store, etc., etc., and loads of concrete paths and walkways.

62

After inspection they were satisfied – they did not know that only the day before the inspection was due there was still no concrete where there should have been. The 'powers-that-be', call it luck or what you will, must have been smiling upon us for there was a concrete lorry with a large whirly container going down the road and the driver stopped when he saw John. John came running indoors and blurted out, "Mum, I've bought two yards of ready-mix concrete for £2 and two dozen eggs." I found the money and he packed the eggs into my little brown carrier and gave it to the driver. That was the last I saw of my carrier, but it was certainly a very good exchange for us!

So, John and I worked ourselves almost into the ground that evening. We shovelled it into the wheelbarrow and laid the garden path, we laid the small area near the bail which also fronted the dairy. That had been a garage from a purchase 'up in the village', and whitewashed inside and cleaned up it was certainly adequate. Oh yes, it had a concrete floor too, so all was well.

That dairy is still there, so is the milking bail, and very useful all the equipment has been.

Sometimes when we were feeding more animals than we needed for milking the pastures would be a little sparse – 'young stock coming on' as most of the farmers used to call the heifers or animals who would not eventually be wanted as milkers. It was then that the aerodrome could prove useful. In the spring and summer many loads of weed-free grass were cut from the aerodrome, and also brought from Kenley Aerodrome in the large trailers pulled by tractors. The route was quite a busy one, all along the Godstone Road and down one of the steep hills leading to the village of South Nutfield and on to the Redhill Aerodrome. Here it all ended up in the grass drier just at the end of our property. That is, if there was time to deal with it and turn it into grass meal.

There were many occasions when that was not possible and the staff would be only too pleased to bring tractor and trailer on to our land so that we could unload for the cows. Many times I have helped to dig it out of the trailer too, from the front right up to the wire! Sometimes it would be only half a trailer load which was really safer for the animals – it was not good for them to gorge themselves on too much rich grass.

These trailers were big with high metal sides like lattice work and if the back had not been undone than the only way in was to climb up over the front. Yes, I did manage it on many occasions.

All that grass drying finished many years ago now, though the main building, patched up many times on the outside, is still just over our boundary. Like our property it is subject to the best and worst that the weather can do and over a long period it begins to show.

For some years all went smoothly with our herd, then the council made a decision to build a 'treatment plant' on the slope up from the stream, taking some land from the aerodrome owners, and wanting to 'run' a pipe line across our fields. They did, of course, and had to screen it off from the animals by wire fencing. Although this was some years ago, I can still see the difference in the ground where their 'filling up' has sunk several times! That strip also grew some very good weeds – the subject of several letters for compensation and eventually a settlement was reached.

The last straw was, of course, the construction of the M23. It went right through fields that we rented 'down the road' and it meant that we would have to sell many animals. John considered and decided to finish milking, taking a job at a neighbouring village. We still had a few animals and were relying on a house cow. John said, "You'll have to do the milking," so I did, after some-trepidation. 'Laurie' was a biggish Jersey bought from a neighbour, and very quiet. We were friends all her life.

15

I've Been 'Had'

I do not remember if the ginger-headed boy with the blue eyes came up to see us before John actually left us to go to another part of the country to work on road construction, staying with Mrs Williams down in Starcross, but he certainly visited us after.

He had a proposition: Could I rear some calves for him? I did and he settled up satisfactorily. He also owned a bull and a few of the remaining animals were loaded and taken to his place for service.

There were several calves born on Brookside after the milking had ceased on a commercial basis, and this young man was extremely helpful in keeping an eye on how things were going, even staying up at Brookside past midnight on purpose to see that everything was all right with the cow.

So I trusted him. I do not now because he had another proposition that his neighbour over at Ockley would be able to purchase any animals I had surplus.

At that time there were, in fact, several which could be sold, so it was arranged that he would come on a certain evening with a cattle lorry, and although I have a list of all the animals he 'persuaded' into the lorry that was the last I saw of them – or him. I telephoned his friend at Ockley some time later and asked how the animals were settling down – poor man thought I was talking through the back of my head – he knew nothing about them.

My thoughts about the ginger-headed young man do not bear repeating – they are not for elegant or genteel reading! Needless to say, he has never appeared again.

Then there was another young man who had two equines. He had the use of land in Kings Cross Lane but was, I heard later, under notice to leave, possibly because he had also acquired ten or twelve young calves to rear. When he was really 'getting pushed' to get out the young stock found a temporary home at Outwood, and after that, well, yes, they came to Brookside in addition to his two good-sized ponies.

I must say he did his share of looking after them, also helping to unload the trailer loads of grass on fields near the motorway. Eventually he stayed with us, but I was not best pleased with him when I found out that he was on holiday and had not even mentioned it. Quite funny how information sometimes comes my way! In this case a lady up in the village wanted to contact him to do some garden work and would I pass on a message as he was on holiday all that week and may be able to fit in her gardening.

His excuse was that he knew I would want him to be busy at Brookside if I knew he was on holiday. Until then I had never really thought of myself as such a slave-driver that I had to be avoided.

When this character knew there was no longer any future in farming with me – how could I trust him again – he became ill and I had the permission of members of his family to sell his stock.

That was another fiasco, for the animals bought by a lady farmer in the East Grinstead direction were not paid for – full of promises when she came with her partner and 'bought' them. She admired the garden and I gave her enough rhubarb for several 'teas'!

So, if anyone ever asks me, "Have you ever been had?" I'll explain just who these characters were!

There have, however, been some very straightforward and helpful people and for their assistance I have been extremely grateful, particularly a family who have been farming for years in Outwood. I can remember leading a fat yellow Jersey animal near 'to her time' back along the road from Outwood and past the 'Prince of Wales', (now 'The Dog and Duck') all the way home.

During these years we did have our own visitors now and again. Lavinia and Derek with Marilyn had moved from Hunters Road in the Tolworth area to Southampton where Derek worked under the Ordnance Survey Office's employ. They had a very nice house there but it was quite a long journey for us to undertake and get back to feed the fowls or do the work we had to do. Therefore, it seemed best for them to visit us and always a pleasure for us to welcome such a visit.

Lavinia was very good at dressmaking and even managed coat-making. I had a blue coat which she made for me and it lasted for years – every time I went to Devon to see to the Bungalow and visit my friends in Crediton or Starcross I wore it. It had a fairly narrow collar of grey fur and Lavinia made me a grey hat to match. I can remember that I thought 'I was the cat's whiskers' – what an expression!

This very evening, as I write, I can hear the traffic on the motorway – the M23 – cutting across farmland which had been peaceful and productive for years. When we came here I do not think there were more than one or two big motorways in the country and they were spoken of with a certain amount of awe! To go on the big motorway was an adventure, an occasion, and now it is so common that few people think twice about travelling on any number of such roads to get from one side of the country to another.

16

Foxes

One night a very long time ago I heard the most awful scream. It was coming from the field across the road – I was glad my husband was too deaf to hear it, for indeed it was weird. I just lay there and prayed! Next day I asked Fred what he thought it could be and he said that a hare will make a realistic scream if in danger from fox or dog! Poor hare, I thought.

I am afraid that we have had several bad experiences at the 'hands' of foxes. Over the years the number of poultry houses had grown to (1) The First House; (2) The Next House; (3) The Swans' House and (4) and (5) a big double shed with a concrete passage up through the middle from which all eggs laid in the well constructed nest boxes could be collected.

A young cock bird was living with his many 'wives' in the first house and one morning I was aware of much noise from there so, of course, I hurried down to the scene. The poor cock bird had been roosting on a proper perch which ended near the wire netting – and his head had been pulled through! Of course he was dead.

There was another time when I was roused from sleep, I believe in those days I used to sleep with 'one eye open' or 'one ear aware of what's going on', and I knew there was no time to spare if I was going to save any of my precious birds. In nightdress and wellington boots I got down the path as soon as I could but many birds were dead and those which remained were too shocked to even think of laying for some time.

I shall never, never forgive foxes for their last predatory

excursion into house No. 5, the lower section. A gentleman up in the village said he had some good pullets on the point of lay but he was finding dealing with the birds a little too much – I believe that he had retired some time ago. So I bought the pullets and was quite pleased with the way they settled down and looked forward to supplying customers again. That is until one morning when I found that they were all dead – a fox had got up on to the roof and somehow dropped in, creating a larder for himself.

Before that the roof looked perfectly sound and how he'd got out again is a mystery. We left them where they were killed and 'he' or 'his many mates' came within a few nights and cleared them all up through the roof again!

I have no sympathy for foxes, as you can imagine. But I think I have been the cause of providing one with a tummy-ache lately – quite inadvertently, of course. I saw traces of rat near the milking bail where I stored the oats for the pony and I put down some rat poison. Next morning it was gone, and the next three or four – I began to think I must have a colony! As I looked over the rails into the hay store there 'he' was – a sleepy fox but just about able to get up and crawl away when he saw me! I called him what he was not christened you may be sure!

I think I have carried a terrible memory of foxes ever since we lived at Bremridge – every year a few special turkeys were reared in a house on wheels which could be moved 'on to the 'errishes' for the birds to pick up any corn left after the sheaves had been stacked and eventually brought in to the farm buildings.

One year all was well until foxy paid a visit and he killed the lot. I saw what remained of the birds – out in Barnsclose – and I knew how frustrated and angry Mum and Annie and Grandma had been, particularly since there was so little time to restock.

When we came to Brookside the hunt worked this area. It all stopped, of course, when the M23 took shape across the fields and meadows.

I saw from my upstairs windows one hunting expedition that ended in triumph for the fox. The hounds made their usual excited barking as they raced down the road and, after a while, still giving tongue and yippering, came back up, followed of course by all the riders.

What they did not know, but what I saw, was a young fox sneaking up the roadside gutter well behind them. That day he lived.

However, there are many animals killed on the roads and a slight bump usually means there is one rabbit less. But Douglas was coming home quite late one night and a fox ran out just at the wrong moment. It was killed, he did what he could and dragged it to the side of the road.

There was yet another killed just outside Brookside Cottage one afternoon. That one was given a decent burial on a spare bit of land inside the aerodrome fence.

The children had guinea pigs as pets, and of course they were safe enough in cages. However, it was difficult to keep cats off the road and I am afraid that there were one or two young animals lost to the car. The last tabby we had must have had nine lives and one or two he used up in climbing a tree right on the verge. The further up he could go the better he was pleased and there were nights when all the persuading in the world had little or no effect and he had to stay there until he decided to come down by himself – and he lived to a wonderful old age.

17

The Front Gate

I have already written that when we came to Brookside the front gate was not in a very good condition although it was adequate at least for the time being.

I was on my own one afternoon, all children in school, husband in London. It was a nice afternoon and the sun shone. As I looked out of the window I saw a stranger just by the gate and he seemed to be making up his mind about coming in. I retreated from sight but I heard him coming up the path beside the cottage.

Nothing for it but to see what he wanted. I was more than a little surprised when he asked if he could have some bread and butter. He said he was walking to Kent, our next county and quite a way off from Brookside.

I left him at the door while I went into the kitchen and cut and buttered some bread. I offered it to him on a plate but he did not seem to know what to do with it – he made no attempt to eat it.

Then suddenly he obviously felt some action was necessary so he grabbed the bread and butter and went off without another word. Weird, I thought.

The next visitor was an official from the local 'Institution' and he asked if I had seen anyone. After my brief description he said, "O Lord, I must stop him," and he also went off, down the road.

We found out in time that people such as this visitor came from The Earlswood Institution and were not meant to be out on their own.

There was another character who was 'on the loose'; he was wearing very heavy hob-nailed boots – sounded like a horse coming down the road. His guard could not have been far behind and caught him somewhere near our cottage by giving him, or showing him, a watch.

Douglas thought it might be better to replace the rickety gate if it meant that it was an invitation to all and sundry to come in.

For quite a while we had no gate but were not too concerned – until the gypsy horses seemed to think that Brookside lawn was perfect grazing material. They also wandered up into the aerodrome several times.

It was then that a local timber firm was approached and proper rails and gate were put in position. Every summer afterwards Douglas treated the wood with the proper preservative and we felt much more secure. Rabbits still invade and there is little anyone can do about them!

Lavinia with Marilyn, me with Janet and Douglas with Jeyne.

My son John.

Jeyne and John.

My daughter Janet Mary.

My son John – peeling potatoes!

Janet's Christening. Back row: Uncle Derek, Auntie Audrey. Front row: Jeyne, Uncle George, me with Janet, Douglas with John, Auntie Venia and Marilyn.

18

The Floods

For hours it had been raining and I knew that floods would probably result. Nobody expected there would be quite so much water – a flood usually meant water was over the road by the bridge, sometimes even across our field bordering the brook.

At such times flood notices did appear but quite often motorists would try to see if they could go through it, sometimes having to reverse all the way up the road from the bridge and turn in our gateway.

The particular one I remember as the very worst happened in the late 1960s I believe. I could find the exact date, it is in one of my diaries but the trouble is that these records are stored in a large box in the annex and just now there is so much furniture from another house stored there that it would take me some time to unearth it, so perhaps you can take my word for it as being then!

In any case, it was before the M23 made its way into this district and the small lanes had quite a different appearance to the wide-ish thoroughfare of today. There was 'quite a corner' to be edged around and ditches which could become full. Even with all the changes which have since taken place the brook still overflows, it's made little difference.

It was in the late morning on a Sunday that the field was under water right up to the road gateway and past it. All the cattle were sheltering well up out of the way – they don't usually mind a few puddles but this, thought the leaders, was ridiculous and 'we beant going near it!'

A motorist left his car and walked into the water, no socks or

f

shoes on and his trouser legs rolled up nearly as far as they would go, but he came back fairly soon, reversed his car up to our entrance – giving the floods "Best!"

John strode off across the fields 'up-brook', coming home some time later with tales of water, water, everywhere!

Being summertime when various organisations arrange their annual outings meant that one unsuspecting driver nearly landed his passengers right in the brook – the front wheels had actually sunk through the sodden verge and had they gone a very short distance further coach and passengers could have been 'up-ended' in the water. It certainly meant hours of waiting before a breakdown vehicle could pull it all back again and, of course, no one could get out!

19

'Uncle' Derek and Lavinia

Of course he was not *my* Uncle – he was my brother-in-law and we were always very good friends. It was always a treat for us – Lavinia and Derek, Douglas and me to meet, either have a meal here at Brookside or visit some local pub. There was 'The Prince of Wales' (after a while renamed 'The Dog and Duck'), 'The Plough' and, some distance away at Puttenham 'The Inn of Good Intent'.

We made a few trips to Andover where Marilyn and Graham now lived. It is some distance from us here at Brookside so trips were not as frequent as one would have wished, but we did go there when it was the anniversary of that so important day when Lavinia and Derek were married. We also went one Christmas – don't ask me which one as off-hand I do not remember, but we met Janet and her two youngsters. It was always a pleasure to visit 'the family' where we were always made so welcome.

'The Inn of Good Intent' was about half way there – I do not know who discovered it – but we met Lavinia and Derek there, were quite impressed with the location, the service, etc., and decided to return again sometime.

Little did we know that we would be returning with a stranger as Lavinia's companion, someone with whom there was a relationship of help and companionship.

Around Christmas in 1992 Uncle Derek had to be in hospital in Southampton. He died there later.

Lavinia was 'lost'. For some time she had been having trouble with failing sight and being so far away there was little we could do to help, so when she told me during one of my weekly calls to her that she had met a very kind gentleman who had realised she was having some difficulty with shopping and who had offered help I felt quite relieved.

Apparently the gentleman, with the fictitious name of John, had been watching her and knew that she had some trouble with shopping – what, I do not know, whether it was selecting goods, trying to get on a bus with a heavy bag, carrying it from the bus stop, or what, anyway he offered to help and Lavinia was very glad of his assistance.

A friendship grew between them. John had a car and when we said that we thought of going to the friendly 'Inn of Good Intent' it was arranged that John would drive Lavinia up so that we could all meet there. You can imagine that Douglas and I were intrigued to meet the stranger. I remember that they were a little late, perhaps they had got lost – perhaps 'he' decided he could not meet us. But no, they did arrive and we all had a very pleasant meal together with friendship between us all.

John had been married before, twice, and had lost both wives to the dreaded illness which overtakes so many women from somewhere about middle age onward. From the first marriage there were several children – one daughter became involved with farming on The Isle of Islay. John and Lavinia went there two or three times, staying for several days.

Perhaps you could say that Lavinia was somewhat of a restless soul – she liked travel and I can remember photographs of far away places which she had visited with Derek, though mainly on the Continent, for I do not remember African, Indian or American destinations being featured or described.

For a while John and Lavinia continued with their separate establishments but eventually her house, where she had lived with Derek for quite a number of years, was sold and she moved in with John full-time.

Her sight had become more of a problem – all the visits to clinics and specialists could not do more than make the latest aids available, perhaps some relief for a while but not a permanent improvement.

Every Sunday morning we used to have a telephone conversation – one week it was my turn to ring her and I would await her call on the following weekend. I began to realise that things were very difficult for her after she described how ill she had felt 'yesterday' and how she had relied on John for assistance.

Scheduled visits to a Nuffield Hospital gave help and hope, at least for a short time and she returned to John again – until the last time.

We received a telephone call from Marilyn saying how ill her mother was and that Graham and their son, Andrew, would collect us on a Sunday morning and take us to Southampton to visit Lavinia in hospital, returning to their home in Andover for lunch.

Andrew and Marilyn came to the hospital with us. Lavinia was in a pleasant room on her own and too poorly to do more than hold my hand. There was no possibility of her being able to speak, but the pressure of her hand spoke volumes; I hope the comfort she received from mine helped.

Apparently the nurses had told Marilyn that it would not be long. She died early on the following morning, between the 25th and 26th September 1995.

Lavinia's Funeral was at Chandlers Ford on the 5th October 1995 – Graham collected us. We are all going to miss Lavinia so much. She was such a definite character, 'A spade was a spade' and not a 'digging instrument'!

We went back to John's house for the family to meet some of Lavinia's friends. John's daughter from his first marriage 'did the honours', welcoming everybody; poor girl had already experienced the two funerals of John's wives, first her own mother, then the second wife, and now Lavinia. I know she said, "I hope I do not need to do this again!"

The clergyman was also a visitor and during conversation he mentioned that on his travels abroad he had met a gentleman from Devon – a very keen birdwatcher – and I had a feeling that I knew who he was talking about. This was confirmed when the clergyman said, "He used to play the organ sometimes, usually hymns."

"Do you mean Graham Madge?" I asked. "I went to school with him, many years ago, of course."

Yes, it was the same, Graham was always known as 'Stanley' in those days.

When he heard of Lavinia's death he composed the following verses and sent them to me – a very valued expression of sympathy:

When we were young Life's road, stretching ahead of us,
Seemed limitless. The end beyond our knowing,
A distance wrapped in timeless mystery,
Beyond imagination.

When we are old, (If by God's Grace we reach that far),
And looking back we see – The journey we have come –
How long that road of many twists and turns
Still seems, yet this is strange – That childhood's
days seem very near, Even if eighty years have passed
Our childhood is as yesterday.

How short a while it seems since I first learnt
To button my own coat, Or tie a shoelace, part my
hair, Or sing a simple song in tune.
Yet now, in age, I scarce recall what I was doing
yesterday, Still less a month, a year ago.

The road of life with all its travelled years
Leads back, it seems, as we approach its end,
Close to the point where we began the journey.
Strange it may seem but it is only right, For when
our earthly road runs out, And we have reached what
seems its end, That end is but a new beginning,
Another stage along the way, That leads us on to God.

So long thy power hath kept me, I once sang,
Now I can sing again with confidence, Sure, sure it
still will lead me on. The Christ who led us on our
way, Even when we faltered and forgot, Still keeps
His promise. I will not forget, will not forsake you.

If we remember this, our sorrow
At the loss of those we love,
Though it may not diminish in our hearts
Yet in our minds it must grow less,
For with our intellect we know
That they have travelled on, Where we,
if we keep faith, one day must follow
To realms of clearer Light,
Of greater knowledge and of keener sight.
                  Thanks be to God.
                  (For Dorinda, October 1995)

I do have news of John from time to time, he always sends a long letter at Christmas.

For a while he was very lonely, but the art classes he and Lavinia had attended together gave him an interest. One of the other students – as elderly as Lavinia and John – sold her house and came to live with him. Eventually also that house was sold and they moved to a more rural location, some distance from Winchester. I think they married.

John's daughter from 'The Isles' went with her family to Australia or New Zealand – I forget which.

Marilyn and I keep in touch nearly every weekend. I say 'nearly' as she is a teacher and of course the school holidays present the opportunity to take long holidays – usually well away from this country. I know that she and Graham have visited many islands, places on the Continent, even one year they went to Norway, another to America.

I am the 'Great' Aunt to their two children – Andrew is married, has a home somewhere in Wales, and Emma works somewhere in the Reading area – something learned and technical.

Life proceeded fairly quietly for some years, Douglas retired from the Civil Service and we took life easily – although he still drove his car, this meant some trips down to Hedgecourt Pond – our nearest seaside!

I still had the cow and the pony – people are somewhat astonished when I tell them (and this is perfectly true) that 'Dorcas' was milking for years after the birth of her last calf – it worked out to be eleven years according to my records – and it was still very good milk. But one morning she did not get up and I knew what I had to do.

It was with a very heavy heart that I had to say 'Good-bye' to her – no more 'rough tongue' licking, no more head over the gate looking for me and avoiding just where that pony might want to go! Thereby hangs another tale, of course, and the wild creature rescued so many years ago because she ran into our property is equally at home here.

20

Sheikah Noora Al Kalifa of Bahrain and Bremridge Farm

Mr and Mrs Thorne were leaving Bremridge Farm, the Devonshire farm of my childhood. They came to live there when Mr Williams decided to go to Starcross, a district right down on the coast. This was where his uncle had farmed for many years at Staplake, having rented the property from Lord Devon.

I had known the Thornes quite well as is evident from accounts in *Under The Hills of Bremridge*. Mr Thorne rented the Brake from me for wintering some of his stock until his financial position necessitated a move away from the area.

As always there was speculation as to who the new owner would be. In time I knew that the new occupant would be Sheikah Noora Al Kalifa of Bahrain. This was in the early 1980s. She is known locally as 'The Princess'; she seems to visit this country for several months at a time but as well as Bremridge she now also owns Trew Farm which comes into the Shobrook Parish. Both farms are high on the hills overlooking villages down in the valleys.

It does not stop there – as other farmers have either sold up or retired so Sheikah Noora has now increased the acreage associated with Bremridge to more than 700 acres. My grandfather always considered that the acreage of the farm was about 130 acres.

She also owns another property 'Sharlands' across the Broxfords road. 'Road' is a misnomer for it is nothing but a lane, and steep in places, particularly above my little properties at

Heath Bridge. It also appears that Sheikah Noora Al Kalifa owns many acres in the neighbouring Upton Hellions Parish, steep hilly fields bordered by narrow lanes. In our day at Bremridge, in the time of the pony and trap or the horse and cart, it was always a relief to round a corner without being confronted by a driver who was just as afraid of the horse and trap as we were of the creature on four wheels.

"When are you coming down again?" This was a question asked many times over the years – 'down' meant going to Devon and staying at Starcross with Mrs Williams and visiting some of her relations. It was my holiday and a very enjoyable quiet one – a rest from farming at Brookside and a chance to catch up with all my Devon friends, in addition to doing any business or actual work in connection with the Bungalow and Cottage at Heath Bridge.

There was Lenore, Dennis, David, Fred and Peter all living within the district and Oriel and her husband near Exeter in the Pinhoe area.

I have made quite a number of trips to Devon over the years, being able to catch up with much news there and 'at home' in the Crediton district. Wherever I went I was always made very welcome and excursions around Devon over the years took in beauty spots, including visits to the north of the county.

Visits to my father were also possible – and enjoyed when we started from Exeter and went to the Midlands, but what a journey in one day!

So it happened that I went to stay with Mrs Williams at Staplake again on Thursday the 10th September, 1987.

I did not know it but I was to go back to Bremridge again and meet the Princess. I do not know why I had a telephone conversation with her – possibly because she had heard I was an adjoining owner – but she invited me to pay her a visit at Bremridge, saying that her driver would meet me in Crediton and take me to the farm.

I thanked her for the invitation and offer of a lift but asked if Mrs Williams and Lenore could come as well in which case we would have our own transport.

So it was arranged, amid much speculation as to how we should behave in the presence of a real live Princess with all of us considering ourselves on the lower rungs of the society ladder of independent farmers.

We need not have worried. The Princess was out with her driver when we arrived but after a few minutes a green Land-rover came into the yard; Sheikah Noora stepped down, greeted us and introduced her driver as Mr Martin Brayne.

I had noticed how different the courtyard had become to the time when I lived there. The stable still existed, though probably not used for horses any longer. The trap house had disappeared but the calf 'boxes' were still across the court and all the other buildings still looked familiar.

Trees bordering the lane had been lost to Dutch Elm disease no doubt, as had the large elm just behind the 'boxes' separating the back court from Barns Close, a field I can remember having a 'cluster' of ricks.

As we walked over the front path between the two lawns I thought of how I learned to cycle there, and since it is not very long it was a case of one foot down every few turns of the wheels.

The front garden where Grandpa had been pleased to grow his early vegetables had lost its high brick wall to the space where vehicles could be parked. Were there still three big tall yew trees on one part of the lawns? I do not remember exactly from that one visit.

As we entered from the front door I noticed at once that the through passage (through to the back door) had been shortened into a convenient hall. It had always been a problem when we lived there because if the front door and back one were open at the same time, there could be breeze or wind enough to make the front door bang and the two small panes of glass in that door would be shattered. I can remember my mother measuring-up, on more than one occasion, for replacement glass and she could put it in herself.

I was able to tell the Princess the history of the little hole fairly high on the wall which was behind our kitchen. It was drilled through so that the flex connecting the wireless loudspeaker could be connected with some kind of 'receiver' in the kitchen, so that if you wanted to listen to the programme – particularly the Church services – you could do so while actually working.

There had been a His Master's Voice wireless in the sitting-room for some time and the vicar, clergyman, or whoever he was, annoyed Grandpa when he was speaking about 'appreciation'. He said, "Do you ever take your wife a bunch of flowers?"

"Flowers," Grandpa hooted and left the room.

I noticed that the dairy passage had disappeared, so the sitting-room was larger than I remembered. Now there are two staircases in this room and the substantial studded door to the back stairs would have many tales to tell if only it could speak. It was due to a fall down the last three steps of the back stairs early one morning that Grandma suffered a broken leg just above the ankle. I know that she was in the Royal Devon and Exeter Hospital for three weeks. There had been some sort of complication but when she was allowed home her bedroom was arranged in the 'end' room across the passage, and I can remember playing 'nursey' to her and making sure that she was comfortable.

You could describe the interval before lunch as a very pleasant half hour. I am sure, too, that there were many memories for the three of us who had spent so many years in the large farmhouse on top of one hill and below another – 'the one to Upton Hellions'.

The dining-room bore no resemblance to the room we used as the big kitchen. The stone floor with the uneven 'dip' near the fireplace had been upgraded and was now covered with a modern facing, an attractive pattern. The dining table had been placed along the wall backing on to the sitting-room whereas ours had always been under the window. The window bench had made a lovely play area when meals had finished and it was only 'the womenfolk' working around the kitchen. Lavinia and I always had horses and traps or carts as well as dolls, a big teddy-bear and a host of small tin toys.

That large kitchen table with the three drawers was used for all sorts of things besides the substantial meals which farmers and their families expected in 'our' day. There was always an ironing blanket not far away and the flat irons were heated beside the open fire: 'irons' because there were always at least two so that when one cooled the other from the fire or hot ashes could be brought into service.

I remembered our large oak kitchen cupboard – the top shelves held everything likely to be wanted in a hurry, always a jar of home made jam or pickle beside the sugar, butter on a dish, a tea caddy, spices, and in the corner of a shelf there was a bottle of some liquid prescribed by the doctor for me because of my awful colds. This liquid had to be painted on the back of my throat – oh yes, I remembered all sorts of things in addition to the everlasting jug of cider on the end of the kitchen table.

No electricity when we lived there – and for some years after until a line was taken across to the farm – so there was a collection of oil lamps and I believe the small ones were housed in the cupboard under the stairs. That became a lovely place for storing all sorts of oddments. If anything was lost (and small enough) it was the first place to be investigated.

The plaster ring in the middle of the kitchen ceiling was still there. Because Grandpa's tea on the kitchen table had the sun playing on the liquid there were reflections which danced and wobbled around on this ring and I remember how they fascinated me.

We could sit right in beside the open fire – lovely in winter. Weakly lambs sometimes shared that space!

Before the meal we were joined by the Princess's two daughters. They might have been early teenagers. I wonder if they remember the three visitors to their home. Mr Braine was also present.

In the early afternoon we had a drive in the Land-rover around the farm, around the fields we all knew so well. Mr Braine was the driver, of course, with the Princess beside him while the three passengers were in the seat behind in a row.

There was another person – a lad from another country – probably India – and it was his job to come from somewhere in the back of the vehicle and open the gates for the Land-rover to pass through. It waited just long enough for the lad to catch up and regain a seat.

I saw Quarry Pit Hill in the distance but we did not go very near it.

Memories returned of going to Hellions Church with Grandma about once a month. We always walked so that you could pick your way over the stones, opening all the gates just wide enough to get through. It was quite different when the pony and trap used that hill because the gate opened back down the hill – it could do no other. Often it was my job to pull the gate open and let it swing into or near the hedge of the adjoining field – Bremridge Close. Usually I did not get back into the trap until it had stopped right on top of the hill. Then we moved off again until the next gateway, and the next. I believe there was still one more and this belonged to Hellions Barton Farm – Jackie Dicker's property. The road here was just a track and often the pony was allowed to take its time through this field while Mum and I enjoyed the children's comic of the day which I think was *Tiger Tims*. on the way home.

It was not often that Lavinia and I were going to Crediton at the same time. In my case it was because I was often home with a cold and my trips involved something which I dreaded – a visit to the doctor.

Later on there were Saturday afternoon journeys to Crediton to fetch a charged up accumulator for the wireless. I think they lasted about a fortnight. The big batteries sat in the window seat in the sitting-room. I do not remember how they were renewed or recharged but they were not replaced for months, maybe a year!

Quarry Pit was an area overgrown with nettles, docks and thistles . . . but that is enough about the past.

We went from the higher regions to the lower fields of the farm in the Land-rover and we saw Ivy Cottage where the Bennetts had lived for many years.

As we came up from there into the field we always knew as Broadpiece with its large oak tree providing shade in summer to any animals who might be in the field, I could not help remembering that one of the cart-horses had been stung by a hornet while sheltering under its large branches. Of course it died, a great loss to any farmer.

Part of this field runs around a curve and it is very steep as it slopes off to the boundary hedge with Little Hill field. Mr Braine was confident of his ability to round the curve and come to no harm but the three of us passengers were not so sure. Sheikah Noora also was plainly worried but I do not know anything about the boy in the back.

Back in the farmyard we said good-bye to the Princess from Bahrain and her driver, thanking her sincerely for allowing us to go back to Bremridge again – always home with all its different memories.

Lenore and Mrs Williams thought there was time to go for a bit of a drive around the area before we would need to go home.

I do not quite remember where we went, it could have been up towards Poughill, but I know we were high on a hill and

85

overlooked Woolfardisworthy in the distance. I think we passed quite near to Down Farm and that was where the Madges had lived – Winnie and Stanley of East Village School days. What a walk! Whichever way you came to East Village from there it was a long way whether it was around Stockleigh English or Copper Oak. Stanley told me once that there was often a lorry going up Cross Hill where the driver had to change gear, which meant slowing down in those days. If they were near enough – and lucky – they held on to the back of the vehicle and had a lift to the top of the hill.

When my sister Lavinia and I were invited to Down Farm we usually walked there but were fetched back home by Mum with the pony and trap, and when 'the little Madges' came to tea at Bremridge Mr Madge would come and collect them.

Happy memories at the end of a very happy day.

21

Douglas in Hospital

To be as deaf as my husband became is a terrible handicap. Yes, I know there are many appliances and aids which can be used to make life a little happier, less of a 'little world shut in to yourself', and I am sure Douglas studied literature where appliances and aids were supposed to give full hearing again. Only they did not!

Many times I have seen him reaching for the little containers on top of the bookcase, inserting the small 'whatever-you-call-it' into each ear and trying to make the best of it.

Perhaps television was his best informative media, at least he could see much of what was portrayed on the screen. He certainly did not watch 'all and everything', but there were some programmes he really did enjoy – "Those funny old men on a Sunday evening," in addition to the Sunday Service, became quite a treat.

He was always very thankful that he could read, and some of his books on religious and related subjects were his valued companions. I am afraid that I cannot even begin to understand them – he said as much more than once!

It was in the early months of summer 2001 that his health really began to cause a problem. His legs and feet began to swell and I noticed that his right leg below his knee was often damp, but he thought little of it, at least for a while until I insisted that the doctor was requested to call.

After a very brief examination a prescription was written for water tablets which the doctor had to take with him to get it 'made up', 'executed' or 'whatever' at Godstone. So, about lunch-time next day a supply of tablets was delivered. They seemed to be very strong tablets, so after a few days I thought it necessary to dilute or reduce the dose.

Things seemed to be getting better, though one night he did not come to bed at all but spent the hours asleep down in the armchair – covered by a rug. After several hours sitting watching him I decided I must go to bed and let the morning come as it may!

Therefore I was extremely relieved to find Douglas up and about in the morning. He had made a cup of tea ready for when I came downstairs.

Days passed, more tablets. They certainly seemed to be working so we were both very hopeful that the worst had passed, that a good recovery could be maintained.

There was one bone of contention between us – we share a double bed and for some time I found every morning all the bedclothes had disappeared over to the floor on his side of it. True, it was supposed to be summer but in England that does not mean you can be comfortable with no more than half a sheet above you – if you are lucky. He said that he did not know what I was talking about – he had not pulled any bedclothes over to his side of the bed.

Through the kindness of a neighbour I was able to get him slippers he could wear – two sizes bigger than his normal ones.

For a while he thought he would stay upstairs and have some breakfast – cereal – there. He found his bedside chair very comfortable. That did not last very long; I knew it would not because he always liked to spend time with the morning paper spread out on the table.

On the 26th July – a Thursday – Douglas was really ill at night. We had spent a quiet evening together, I had taken the dog out fairly early and the television supplied some entertainment though I do not remember seeing a particularly enthralling programme.

I had given him something to read – an article I knew he would find of interest – and I handed him his spectacles. He did not put them on but just fingered them, so I said, "What is the matter, dear?" He did not answer and I went round the table to him, putting my arm gently round his neck, and I noticed his eyes had turned blue instead of being their usual brown. He still did not say a word. I thought I had better get the doctor.

The telephone rang – and rang – so obviously the 'emergency' number was not manned. A few minutes later I tried again, with the same result. Then I telephoned the police to get an ambulance.

It was quite a while before I heard ambulance sounds in the distance – and they passed this house. The name Brookside Cottage was not easy to see in the dark. Eventually they found us and began treating Douglas immediately – yes, he had to be moved to hospital as soon as possible.

There were two girls, very efficient in their black trousers and yellow tops – they lowered him gently to the floor, but I could not watch what happened – for one thing I had a worried black dog to hold and pacify and for another I could not understand any treatment.

They brought their stretcher into the kitchen, the patient was assisted on to it and then wheeled out through the scullery to the drive and into the vehicle.

"Ring up in the morning," were their parting words.

What would I find, I wondered, as I dialled the East Surrey Hospital next morning after I had taken the dog out and seen to the pony down by the milking bail. So it was a little comfort when a calm voice just said, "Mr Rowe is still with the doctor and has not been shifted to a ward yet – perhaps you can ring up later."

I did, of course, and heard that he had been put in the Meadvale Ward, "Yes, he can be visited this afternoon, any time after 2pm."

I telephoned a neighbour who lived down the road and around the corner, and she offered to take me to the East Surrey and leave me there while she did some shopping.

When the geography of such a building – large but very modern – is unfamiliar then it is more than likely one goes to the wrong entrance, so we went to the main doors. My neighbour went her way to do her purchases and I spoke to a receptionist and asked the way to the Meadvale Ward. She looked at me and said, "I'll get you a wheelchair."

"Wheelchair," I said, "I can walk it."

To which she replied, "It is rather a long way. Wait for a wheelchair. Sit down if you like."

There were other people around – seemed to be a clinic day with mothers with their infants in their arms – so I sat and waited and wondered what I should find when I actually saw my husband. That receptionist was quite right, and the young man pushing the wheelchair cornered this way and that – I certainly would have been lost. Yes, wheelchairs are quite comfortable!

At last the final corner was turned, a slight incline, carpeted, and I was left at the reception desk of the Meadvale. A nurse took me to Douglas's cubicle down a passage with several doors opening off to the right – other cubicles containing very sick people behind each one.

There, in No.5 I believe, was Douglas, sitting up in bed but obviously very poorly. He seemed to be wearing some sort of mask and could not speak to me. Apparently he had been given a blood transfusion. There were small traces of blood on the foot of the bed, as if the tubing had been interfered with. No doubt he did not realise what was happening.

I do not know whether he could appreciate the view from his window. This looked out on to a garden full of tall flowers between shrubs – quite a pleasant outlook.

Douglas could not speak to me, all we could do was to hold hands.

On my way out of the Meadvale I saw the Sister – a very busy lady – and she wanted to take all the details of our house in case he could be home again within a short time. Seeing how he was during my visit I thought 'What a hope!' I gave her all the information she asked for – until she said, "What are your stairs like?" to which I replied:

"They go up and they go down."

This is as I have always thought of them since the house was at its commencement two farm cottages. When they were made into one dwelling the stairs in each were joined by a landing – perhaps 'joined into a landing' would be better to describe it. Therefore you could go up or down either way, to one side of the house or to the other!

'What help would I have at home?' We had not needed extra help, living fairly quietly as a retired couple, at least during the last few years.

It was obvious that 'Sister' thought he would be returning home – a glimmer of hope for me. She called for a wheelchair for me, so it was round this corner and that but even I noticed that it was not the same journey as I made from the entrance. I came to the outside world at quite a different entrance, or exit.

The 'wheelchair boy' was in no hurry to go back again, so he talked behind me – to the back of my head. I learnt a little about the hospital workings but I do not think anyone would envy him his job and some of the tasks he would have to undertake.

So I waited, and I waited. I knew that I would be collected but I began to think shopping was taking a long time. Like me, my neighbour was unfamiliar with the layout of the East Surrey, had gone to our point of entry and had discovered that I could be at the entrance down the road near the car park and eventually found me.

My next visit I arranged by taxi and locked the doors of Brookside and waited, and waited near the railings bordering the lawns – and waited. I knew I had plenty of time but I had not expected the driver to go on until he had discovered he was actually in the next parish – Outwood. I was delivered to the nearest entrance but it was still a good walk to the Meadvale, I had memorised the route of the second wheelchair!

Douglas was better, he was sitting up in bed and was so pleased to see me; he still could not talk but at least we could 'hold hands' and look at one another.

I managed to visit him in the East Surrey nearly every other day but I must say it was a great relief and comfort to me when. my eldest granddaughter came up from Horsham with her little car. She had only recently learned to drive but was very pleased she had passed her test to become a qualified driver – so was I!

The staff of the Meadvale Ward were very puzzled by Douglas's treatment of his bedclothes, for as soon as he could get out of bed and sit in his chair he stripped sheets and covers right down to the mattress leaving them at the foot of the bed.

I explained that he had always done that at home. In fact, ever since his Army days, his bed was 'opened' in the morning. Sometimes made up again by him sometimes by me if I went upstairs before he had finished the paper in the morning or was out walking the dog! So, even in hospital habit dies hard.

A week or so later one of the nurses told me that, "Mr Rowe was a naughty boy – he wandered." He had, been found out in the car park belonging to that part of the hospital. They had to watch him. Busy as they always were I felt it was something extra they could well have done without.

On one visit at about four o'clock in the afternoon he was

having a meal, with a nurse standing guard beside his trolley. When he saw me he was so delighted he clapped his hands high in front of him. On another visit he kept pointing to his feet, so I said, "What is the matter with them?"

He said, "Socks," as clearly as possible, and, of course, I went to his locker and put them on him.

We had a few outings together – the room at the far end of the passage past all the small ward or cubicle openings was well furnished with comfortable chairs. I would think it was a room used for meetings. Anyway, a walk to it and a sit down seemed to be appreciated by some patients, Douglas included, although he seemed to be asleep very soon.

I think it was too much to expect him to recover from the disaster of his own making. On my next visit a nurse was obviously on the look-out for me and she invited me to sit for 'a little chat'. Apparently, Mr Rowe had locked himself in the bathroom and had turned the taps on. How flooded everything became was not explained but his slippers were wet so would I take them home to dry. He was left wearing socks – and slipped down.

He was back in bed with the rails in place forming a cot. Obviously his fall had set him back for days and days. He was groaning and miserable, although he did try to turn himself over now and again. We held hands just for a few minutes – I wondered if ever he would be out of bed again.

On my next visit he was sitting in a wheelchair which seemed somehow to be locked, stationary. He was obviously a little better than he had been at my last visit which had filled me with foreboding and unhappiness.

Then I heard a beautiful voice – I could scarcely believe it but the patient in the next cubicle was a lady singing hymns; well known church hymns. I think I shall always remember that voice and at that time it was wonderfully comforting. One of the nurses told me that she had sung in a church choir – she was blind now. I was scarcely prepared for what happened next – a piercing scream from that cubicle and the nurses running to help her.

A gentleman of about my husband's age was walking up and down the corridor. He stopped at 'our' door, held it open and said, "I've lost me bearings," two or three times. Then he wandered off again – I could not help him. I did not know where he came from but I knew a nurse must soon find him.

There was another character at the hospital, and she wanted to see me or any relative of Mr Rowe's – oh yes, she did, and she was after finding out what chances there were, when Mr Rowe was well enough, of course, of getting him shifted into a 'Care Home' and what were the financial means of support.

This lady had come to this country from South Africa and I had a telephone call from her one morning to enquire if I had made any progress or what was the present position. I do not think she could have been aware of the 'set-back' which had occurred and that it would now be some time before Mr Rowe would be well enough to leave hospital.

My visits I timed to end before six o'clock, so that I could walk to the east entrance and wait for my taxi – prearranged for that time, of course.

Several evenings I waited much longer. The view took in car parks, part of a golf course, the country around and what seemed to be a tower – The Earlswood 'Home' for unfortunates, now no longer so used. But I remember it for quite a different reason – it had enough ground to provide hay from standing grass and one year we were able to buy it.

It was after John had left home. After all this time I have forgotten the exact circumstances and I do not know why it had been offered to us, but it was, acres of 'standing grass'. We possessed a very good mowing machine – I had bought it at a farm sale some time before for cutting grass for hay in our own fields, and at that time the tractor was in good condition and could be relied on away from home. We also had the other equipment for turning and 'rowing up', normally used only for a few days in summer.

I do remember going to The Royal Earlswood once by car and the dog accompanying us took exception to one of the inmates who came over, possibly a little too near, so there was some furious barking for a while!

It must have been from this 'Institution' that the man walking to Kent and asking for food had called at Brookside not long after we had gone to live there. He must have been very keen to get away because it is quite a long walk from The Royal Earlswood to Brookside, and still quite a good way from Kent.

From the east entrance to the East Surrey Hospital it is

certainly a landmark dominating the surrounding countryside. There seems to be a golf course near and I saw people out walking their dogs, and a very good view up over the hills to the north. I usually had plenty of time to wait for my taxi but once or twice I had too much time and it was then that I remembered the work with the hay. The taxi was late.

I remembered we must have borrowed – or were offered – the big red trailers from the aerodrome for bringing the hay home and I can remember lying on top of a load from Earlswood to Brookside and the journey involved going through part of Redhill and going up Redstone Hill, then turning into the hill leading down to the valley – and home.

After visiting the hospital on the 11th September, I discovered that the taxi driver was from another country; Sri Lanka – not the first one from that country taking the job of a taxi driver and usually their command of the English language was, at least, fair. When this particular driver started talking about something in New York without giving more information than 'thousands keeled' I did wonder what he was talking about. He proved to be only too right.

Well, the visits to Douglas in the Hospital went on. Lucy and Kathy came in when they were staying near enough, and there was also a visit from Marilyn and Graham all the way from Andover.

Then, one afternoon a nurse at their information desk said that they had moved Mr Rowe into another ward.

Here he had several companions, most of them either being fast asleep or just 'nodding off'. The gentleman in the next bed was more than partly hidden by curtains and he was obviously very thin and ill.

Jeyne and John came, with Naomi too as she had not seen Grandad for some time – several years, in fact.

The visit was over, and as we turned to say 'Good-bye' Douglas was making efforts to get out of bed and, I suppose, come too. Of course he could not – I doubt he would have been able to stand. Back at the information desk I suggested that he needed attention and a young male nurse immediately went to him.

My next visit was my last for I could see that he had deteriorated very considerably. He could not even try to say anything and I noticed the colour of his legs had become very dark, as if they were cold. He was still being well looked after and the male nurse from far overseas covered his feet and legs again. He was one who came round every afternoon with the medicine trolley and I still have a picture of him handing out a tablet to Douglas when he was in the cubicle ward and making sure he had it by giving him a drink afterwards. He knew that I was upset when Douglas was so poorly after his excursion to the bathroom when he turned the taps on, and as I looked out of the window he came over and put an arm around my shoulder for just a moment.

There was a telephone call from the hospital very early next morning but I did not take it for I had gone out to feed the pony and take 'Girlie' for her early morning stroll. The hospital then telephoned Jeyne in Horsham and Donna, one of their particular friends, drove her and John up to the hospital.

Jeyne said she is sure that Douglas had 'passed away', although 'only just'.

Of course, I do not know what her thoughts were but I can confirm that, although a little strict at times, he had been a very good parent. He had provided a good home for us all and had produced a very good cheque for each of the three children for Christmas and for birthdays.

I forgot to mention John's visit from Yorkshire. He came down and stayed at Brookside Cottage for about a week, going in to see Douglas with me two or three times.

All the arrangements for the funeral had to be made so there were many telephone conversations with members of the family.

Our vicar from South Nutfield came to see me one afternoon – I think we talked about everything except death. He said he would be prepared to be in charge at the crematorium for prayers and to say what I should like Douglas remembered for, unless I would like to undertake to say something myself.

Shades of East Village again and the chapel, so I knew what I had to do. Douglas never liked what he termed 'pomp and ceremony' and I knew that the few simple sentences I had already thought out would be very sincere and adequate.

Also 'Thought for the Week' in the *Daily Mail* of September 24th, 2001, the day Douglas passed on, said, 'I, I am he that comforts you," Isaiah 51-12.

October the third was warm and sunny, Kathy drove me in her

little grey car. Marilyn and Graham came over from Andover. Janet and Lucy, Jeyne, John and Naomi and Donna, our John (from Yorkshire), Robbie and – much appreciated, two members of the Nutfield Conservation Society were standing with Peter under the shade of a large tree awaiting the arrival of the hearse.

Apparently Robbie, Kathy's brother, had only just 'made it' from Burgh Island by telephoning Janet and arranging for her to pick him up. Robbie seems to have tremendous good luck in being able to get around the country by 'lifts'.

The only family member not able to be present was Janet's son, James. He was in the Army and believed to be out of the country. John (from Yorkshire) represented the members of his branch of the family.

The service was as simple as Douglas would have liked, and as the coffin slowly slid away behind the closing curtains, no doubt each of us paid a silent tribute to Douglas, with thanks for a good home and security, given for all the years of his life with his care and devotion.

The next stop was at 'The Plough' where dinner for us all had been arranged. Marilyn and Graham soon had to leave to fulfil a prior engagement.

Janet had to get Lucy to Redhill for her train to Reading and I went home with Kathy and Peter.

I was reminded of the time we went to Uncle George's funeral at a crematorium.

George's visit was on a bitterly cold day. The weather seemed to add considerably to the feelings of sorrow and depression – sorrow for being so helpless and not being able to do more than weep and depression generally for the loss of someone dear to you, someone for whom you cared. There was also the question of could we have done more to help him?

The flowers we had to leave behind looked as cold as we felt – Jeyne and John and Douglas and me. They took their place between a beautiful wreath and a cushion heart shaped tribute.

Jeyne and John went back to Horsham by train and Douglas and I returned to Brookside by car – neither of us saying anything on the journey.

I felt the contrast between that visit to the crematorium and the one on which I had just been quite keenly. Although it was October when Douglas was laid to rest it was a lovely day, when

Me with Janet, Jeyne and John.

Josie the cow.

Abdulla Felaj
who stayed at
Brookside Cottage
whilst training at
Sandhurst.

Major H Hassan –
another resident
at Brookside
Cottage.

Mutlac and Akash
on one of their visits
to London.

My daughter Jeyne.

Douglas, me and Jeyne, with Girlie, May 1999.

we were glad to stand under the shade of the tall trees to await the coming of the hearse.

I am not going to tell you what my tribute to Douglas actually said – I feel it is too personal – but I ended it with the following lines:

Three Volumes

Life is a book with volumes three,
The Past, the Present, the Is To Be,
The Past we've read and put away
The Second we are living day to day.
The last of the Books is Volume Three
And is kept from sight,
God keeps the key.

h

22

Douglas's Cousin Archie

One member of the family who was missing at the funeral for Douglas was Douglas's cousin Archie.

It was many years ago when I saw Archie. He had come to visit us with his wife, Hilda, who was then an invalid. She has since died so Archie is on his own at Plymouth. I know he belongs to a club where walking over Dartmoor is one of their aims and pleasures.

We have kept in touch with the occasional letter, usually at Christmas or if there was anything special happening; always a pleasure.

Apparently Archie had been taught to swim when he was a good sized boy by Douglas, something he never forgot!

When he knew Douglas was ill in hospital there were several telephone calls between us. I knew his sympathy was very real and since he had been a chemist by calling be was very aware of what I might expect to happen.

Kathy, Jeyne's daughter, probably had more contact with him than other members of the family could have as she was studying at Seal Hayne and living in Devon. She was also able to make contact with Mrs Phyllis Stevens, the widow of another cousin, in Drewsteignton. The Rowes' roots are certainly in Devon and round about the moor.

It was Archie who told me about the family grave at Efford and the possibility of adding Douglas's name in due course. So it seemed only natural that the family should decide that Dartmoor should be the resting place of the ashes to be scattered in due course.

Janet in Cornwall, and her Lucy, Kathy and Peter, Archie and Robbie Azopardi all met on the appointed day and walked up to the Tor which had been one of Douglas's favourite haunts as a schoolboy.

There were some snapshots, taken by Peter I expect, showing the ashes being scattered and blowing about in the wind, so Douglas rests on Dartmoor – whither the wind takes him.

Archie was able to make arrangements for Douglas's name to be included on the family stone and asked me what I would like as an inscription; it had to be fairly short so I suggested 'Rest in Love'.

Archie was quite concerned that I was living on my own up at Brookside. Of course, the house is well away from the village of South Nutfield, and his suggestion that, in time, Janet should come up from Cornwall and live with me was taken seriously and eventually acted upon.

Janet moved in with Bryn her little dog who became a good friend of Girlie, and her nine cats. She does the feeding and looks after them all!

23

The Redhill Aerodrome

When we came to Brookside – in 1955 – there were two wartime cottages quite near our property, one was occupied by Mr and Mrs Barnes, a very friendly couple. Mr Barnes was very fond of his garden, flowers, vegetables and shrubs. I think the apple trees were planted by them, very productive and much appreciated.

I have forgotten the name of the other couple; there were several changes of tenancy for this one, ending with Mr and Mrs Jones (Taffy).

There were also several structures of the wartime variety and over the years they have been dismantled and completely disappeared. In fact, we have benefited to the extent of receiving some building materials which have been very useful in constructing animal enclosures or fodder stores.

Once, when I was in Devon seeing to the Bungalow, my husband had a very worried call from Mr Barnes – 'Mrs' had collapsed. I am afraid that she died. Mr Barnes was not able to remain on his own and his daughter found him suitable sheltered accommodation away from this area.

Before long Mr and Mrs Jones went to live in Top Nutfield and this meant that both cottages were soon demolished, although the big fir tree and the apple trees remain. Every spring/summer there is a wonderful show of daffodils, now spreading a little further than the original gardens. For several years I used to go in when it was quiet and collect some of the apples which fell down – almost tumbled into my lap! Then came the rabbits and every apple was nibbled, so I 'gave them best' which is, I believe, the right expression for letting them win!

Then there were rumours. New owners wanted to make it into an aerodrome capable of doing great things, providing services in connection with Gatwick, and eventually there was a Public Inquiry. 'Brookside' would have been swallowed up, in fact the house would have been right under the runway, even Crab Hill Lane may have been put into a tunnel. Oh yes, the owners or would-be developers had got it all worked out.

Before the inquiry ended local people were invited to have their say, 'Submit a paper' in other words. I spoke up, yes, shades of East Village Methodist Chapel were always in the back of my mind: 'You can do it and you must'. If I can locate my 'paper' I will include it.

My husband had already been approached by somebody from the firm who would be negotiating our sale price – he was not keen to sell, to have to move with all that it would mean.

So we were very glad 'the Minister' turned it down!

So everything went quiet for a while. For some years there had been an exhibition on the aerodrome which meant the provision of a very large structure which I believe was known as a tent, but it was much more elaborate and weather resistant for it had to cater for 'tribes of visitors' inspecting whatever was on display.

There was one year when this large tent was built just across the lower part of the aerodrome, so we had an excellent view of all the comings and goings. It was a great pity that the weather decided to be inclement for there was a downpour on the visitors and their cars, and on leaving some of them got stuck in the mud. I know that help was on hand in the shape of the aerodrome tractors.

Another 'activity' out on the aerodrome is the training of some firemen. I do not know how often this takes place or whether it is always the same headquarters availing themselves of the facilities – if you can call it such.

I have seen – and watched – a collection of firemen in their uniforms over the other side of the aerodrome near the little track which leads to the aerodrome agricultural buildings. There is also a brook at the end of a tunnel the width of this portion of aerodrome. These unfortunate firemen are encouraged or goaded into the tunnel and told to walk to the end. What they do not know, though, its where the end is, for blackouts have been placed over the end of the tunnel and – so I was told by someone who had witnessed what happened – the poor unfortunates nearly always land in the water!

One day in summer long long ago I walked to our garden hedge and looked over and there was a man, a man who took to his heels and fled. I have no idea of what he was doing, just standing still and watching. I think I might have said 'hello'; he certainly did not answer, he took to his heels and disappeared through the hedge – it was after the gateway to the cottages had been 'stopped up' so it would not have been easy for him to escape without several scratches. Very soon I heard him start his car and he was gone – up the road I think. He was wearing grey trousers and a short sleeved shirt, no hat. As far as I know he did not visit the area again; there were no sequels of any sort, but I wondered what he had been 'up to' – was he connected with the aerodrome and planners?

24

The Public Inquiry

When a local council says 'no' to some scheme which a developer dreams up to make use of some existing facility or to create something alien to the wishes of the local people both of which would alter – for ever – the character of a district then the matter usually goes to appeal or to Public Inquiry.

Thus it was on the morning of the 10th March 1992, the two sides were meeting to put their case under the precise and careful control of the Inspector. For the duration of any inquiry the Inspector is allowed to 'play God' in the quiet and almost hallowed atmosphere of the Council Chamber.

The Chamber itself was probably more oval than round with a very unusual ceiling, sort of pyramid shaped with darker material at the top in the centre – possibly for ventilation, and the lights had an arrangement all of their own. Smallish bulbs coming from the base of the pyramid mounted on long horizontal fittings – 'sticks' – and stopping just short of the centre, wires holding the middle ends.

There did not seem to be any windows at all, though the wooden reeded 'shutters' might have covered windows. They were, possibly, covering a panel of names or just for decoration. The rows of light oak glass topped tables were shaped to fit into the large body of the room; four rows I believe I am right in remembering, and each table had a very comfortable armchair on easy swivelling castors. Every table had been provided with a very convenient 'cubby-hole' for ladies' hand-bags, macks folded up and scarves. Very convenient, indeed.

I think I can describe the colour of the armchairs as 'fawny-pink'. There was a carpet, of course, plain, without pattern, but the whole room presented a feeling that money had not been spared in any way when fitting it out.

The Inspector's rostrum was raised, not to any great height, possibly about three steps. This particular Inspector was, I should say, on the wrong side of middle age, but with, no doubt, a wealth of experience of inquiries. Slightly bearded, slightly bald, dark suited, he sat behind his desk with a wealth of papers and maps and even a photo album all to hand. He had a companion sitting beside him. His presence was explained as another Inspector listening but taking no part in this inquiry, he was just observing – learning, perhaps, I thought.

There seemed to be six or seven male individuals going to do their best to persuade the Inspector the scheme they were supporting would do no harm to neighbours or to the district. Their 'leader' was a thin fairly young man, with a young beard, darkish, in a dark suit. I noticed his hands were those of a 'townie'. They had never seen hard work and probably pushing a pen was about all the exercise they had.

The other group, of course, were the people who wanted to convince the Inspector to let things 'bide as they be' and say 'No,' 'No more traffic, no more cars, no car park, no B1 use of the Red Barn.'

At 10 o'clock precisely the Inspector spoke and outlined the precise manner in which he was going to take evidence, how the developers would state their case first, how everything had to be copied so that all sides were aware of exactly what the case for – or against – consisted of, what it was all about in other words!

But, oh dear, oh dear, he was speaking so quietly that if pins had been dropped the sound of them falling on the carpet would have deadened the quiet voice! One certainly had to pay attention to hear the words and to understand their meaning.

He wanted the names of any interested persons who desired to speak and eventually I had to stand and say I would. He seemed to find my name interesting – Mrs Dorinda Rowe, and address, etc.

I knew I was all right, I had a letter I could read – a copy of which he had and so had the 'other side', but what had I let myself in for I wondered?

The other side's leader started – a Mr Phillips – and there were plenty of 'Sirs' thrown in as he outlined his case and asked if he could call his first witness. Again, I was nearly on the point of saying I was deaf for he talked so quietly it was extremely difficult to hear! He had copious written notes in a loose-leaf file and I thought that we'd be there forever if he had to go through every page! The answers he received from his first witness were given in an equally quiet voice, so I am afraid that all his technical arguments were lost on me! I did catch something about a gypsy site or cemetery being uses allowed in the Green Belt. I wondered why he dragged those uses in!

The Inspector did ask eventually whether everyone could hear what was being said – to which I blurted out, "Only just about!" Mr Phillips reminded 'Sir' that there was a public address system installed – to which 'God' replied that he would rather not make use of one so perhaps we could all move nearer. We did, one row.

I could not return to the Inquiry for the afternoon session, but I knew what I must do. I must write another letter, and so I did, concentrating particularly on the traffic problem. I took some carbons, but not enough, so there had to be some more provided at the Council Offices. Apparently easily done.

At just about 2 o'clock on the afternoon of the 11th I was in the Council Chamber. I had had time enough to study the diagrams around the walls, the lay-out of the car park for either 80, or 58, or 49 cars. There was some ground left over – what was to be its future?

Mr Phillips began questioning a Mr Finney – another quiet voice! A voice with gaps of silence in between while he studied, diagrams on the profile of the road, the effects of taking out some of the hill, etc., etc. The amount of traffic likely, etc. I certainly could not follow some of his reasoning and the Inspector would have had to be mighty clever to do so.

Of course, besides the would-be developers and the protesters there was a third 'degree' – the Council Solicitor, a tall, fairly young lady, married, I noticed, as evidenced by the ring on the appropriate finger, and her assistant, and they had papers and diagrams and reference files making quite a pile; when not in use these were parked on the table of the row behind them. There were more people at the Inquiry on the Wednesday afternoon as interested parties had been given to understand that was when they could put their case. I met several friends I had not previously seen for some time, but of course, there was little time to do more than just acknowledge each other. With the same painstaking thoroughness as when the proceedings had begun the day before, questions – quiet questions – were put by the Council Solicitor. Quite beyond me to hear or to understand, so I made a decision. No matter what they all thought, they would hear what I had written. I remembered how when I had given my name and address all the pairs of eyes of the opposition had turned 'like a whip-top' in my direction.

I remembered something else, too. I remembered a Public Inquiry many years ago where evidence had been given, but too quickly so that the force of the remarks had probably been lost – and I remembered East Village Chapel where I had first quaked and shaken and spoken in public! Pieces of poetry in broad Devon, "You'm as good as the rest of 'em and there's nort to be afraid of – so git on and do it!" So when the Inspector invited my submission I moved forward with my papers. I read my letter, aloud, slowly and carefully and I could feel 'the eyes'. Mr Phillips was asked by the Inspector if he wished to question me; he declined. I have come to the conclusion that any witness with a fool-proof case, or evidence, does not become subject to the other side questioning – I suppose they thought there was nothing to be gained, perhaps more to lose.

Home again, and work to do, and I forgot all about the Inquiry, temporarily, but that night I had a dream – a silly sort of dream where I was in a room sitting behind a row of boys, possibly about ten years old. Someone with me said, "What are you doing?"

I had been staring at them and I replied, "I am measuring the size of their ears."

25

The Public Inquiry Inspector and the Outcome

I have now seen several of these gentlemen and they seem to be cast in a very similar mould. I suppose they did all start off as being babies who became little boys enjoying all the things which children do enjoy, but they are certainly making their mark in the world as adults. It is difficult to imagine what their school days were like but of one thing I am sure – they were all well taught, in other words, whether by the affluence of their parents or through their own efforts, they received a good education!

Each Inspector wears a dark suit, black or very nearly so, although years ago I did encounter one with a dark navy suit. Invariably, there is a very white shirt and a discreet tie, certainly nothing loud or flashy. The initials following the name of an Inspector mean that, even after school, he has studied well, taken exams and been successful. What pride he must feel when he is properly addressed with all of them!

Speaking of Inspectors in the plural – they are all serious creatures – I have never really seen a smile and a genteel laugh would be beyond them, one would not expect it nor would one get it! On the other hand, although Inspectors have impressed a point quite firmly it is always with courtesy. Sometimes there has been a slight show of impatience, of resignation perhaps, while some very quietly spoken 'expert' has read from a long paper on technical points or found it necessary, no 'essential' to indulge in a very detailed statement.

The Inspectors are always writing, they make notes on

everything, each-section or facet of the problem as it is being discussed, although the facts must have been supplied to them well before the inquiry. They always use a black fountain pen laced about with gold, quite an expensive pen I should imagine. Sometimes there is a gold watch just about visible as an Inspector reaches out for a document – and what a pile of papers must be collected before an end to each inquiry – even a comparatively minor one.

After the hearing at the inquiry – or even if it is a written inquiry instead of one where both sides are present – then the Inspector really has a task to sift through all the evidence and to come to a conclusion that is within the framework of the planning laws, so, no doubt, he starts writing again. Perhaps he feels as every shorthand typist does when faced with pages and pages of notes. I wonder if he has a glass of sherry to lighten the task a little – perhaps even something a little stronger, but nothing to excess. I should think he would practice moderation in all things, his trim figure would testify to that.

Finally, he has to write his letter with his conclusions. Upon that will rest the future of houses, of alterations, of developments of all kinds, some quite small but they come within the power of the Local Councils to say 'No', while the would-be developer considers the Inspector could give permission for what they want.

In a very important case even the Inspector will submit his evidence and conclusions to 'The Minister' with a recommendation. The Minister's decision is the ultimate.

So it was with the Public Inquiry into the plans published by a group of developers hopeful that they would receive permission to ruin the neighbourhood of the Redhill Aerodrome by intensifying activities there and turning a green-field aerodrome into a concrete waste. There is also much that goes with such a development which is undesirable; loss of trees and countryside to accommodate traffic from the M23, and there has even been the suggestion that some local roads might have to be put into a tunnel to keep down noise from affecting radar installations. A bund will mask motorway noise, but it cannot hide the sound of a police siren!

The outcome of this inquiry was decided by the Minister and he turned it down – thank goodness!

I've had some disturbing news just lately – with all the space which aerodromes need apparently the question of whether Redhill Aerodrome could be developed to accommodate some of the flying monsters has been asked. The owners would be only too pleased to acquire the Brookside acres, demolish the house, build runways and even make a connection to the M23 for the use of the motorist.

I did hear an opinion that because of the slopes and lie of the land it would not be possible to have really big aircraft here at Redhill, but I expect that will not stop the developers from having a try. It is not just us down here on the Outwood road who would suffer, areas on the other side would be only too well aware of the flying monsters, even perhaps having to close the local school.

There are Tree Preservation Orders on the Oaks across the road, but would that save them? At the moment it is the preserve of the wild animals, squirrels in the branches, rabbits and birds along the roadside ditches. There was talk before of putting Crabhill Lane into a tunnel and what a hell of a noise would be created as the big monsters taxied around and flew off!

The aerodrome was supposed to be safe from further development until about 2020 (something) was reached, but is it? One wonders.

26

Some of the People I Knew

I am sure the whole village knew the people I am going to make a few remarks about, and the first one is Miss Chandler. Every month she is remembered when people in Nutfield and, indeed, much further afield, receive their copy of the *Nutfield Link*, the village magazine which she began in 1974.

I had the pleasure of several long conversations with her when I took her the eggs she was expecting. She was a very interesting lady and even at quite an age, when most people are thinking of retiring completely, she took a trip overseas by aeroplane.

Of course, as long as *The Link* is produced her name will be familiar to many, but the pleasure of knowing her is a bonus.

Then there were the Deacons. For many years I knew Doris and Dick. Miss Deacon came to us for eggs often on her way home from her job 'somewhere across the aerodrome'. She drove a little blue car and was always very polite. She was very artistic.

Dick was very concerned with the environment and it was through him that I also became associated with The Nutfield Conservation Society, soon after the Public Inquiry concerning the Redhill Aerodrome.

No one could take more trouble to get everything completely accurate than Dick did. He would think about problems very carefully before he took any action. We had something else in common – he had been stationed in Exeter either during, or just after, the war and knew the area well.

To grow old and to be able to look back and appreciate the value of one's friends is a blessing indeed.

Then there were the Dickensons – Eddy and his dad, also his uncle who was interested in fancy birds and I do mean the feathered variety.

There were times when we had to trade in eggs – either Mr Dickenson was able to buy our surplus or, when we were awaiting the hoped for production of the last batch of young pullets, we could supplement our stocks from his supply.

It was always a pleasure to visit his store up at Kentwyns – a happy character.

A very long time ago I saw a 'Death Notice' in one of our local papers. It was a tribute to the late Major B. B. Williams, recently living in Wales. This was the Mr Williams who used to deliver our animal food and whose twin brother died in the war.

I believe he had his own smallholding in Wales, or at least a country cottage with a very large and productive garden, for he was not a person to be idle, he would have an interest in everything.

I know that his children – all three – have now married and probably have families of their own. Life moves on and one loses touch; the years seem to pass very quickly when one gets older.

Sometimes it is difficult to remember what I was doing yesterday but the memory of outstanding characters such as Major B. B. Williams can be recalled in an instant.

As far as I know he was not related to the family in Devon, the Williamses, who took Bremridge when Grandpa died. This family and our family have always been friends, and still are.

The expression about 'ships that pass in the night' when applied to such friends as I have had is in no way appropriate. Quite a few have already 'passed on' and one day it will be my turn because no one lives for ever.

Talk of war again now – how many more people will be left without their brothers?

27

Our Young People

As you would expect, our 'young people' became interested in the opposite sex in due course and thereby hangs a tale – maybe not one but many – of the problems of dates, meetings or outings which all seemed to be very respectable and in line with the times.

Our eldest, Jeyne, became 'Mrs Azopardi' up at our local church in February 1977. She looked lovely in a white dress and all that goes with it and John looked to be her perfect partner, very tall and straight.

They had their first home in Horley, sharing a house with an elderly lady. Poor old soul became ill and Jeyne was called upon to give what comfort she could – and did.

That period in Horley also saw the birth of Kathy – I think she has grown into a beautiful young lady and, indeed, so helpful to her poor old grandmother when my husband was in the East Surrey Ward at our local hospital.

Jeyne's next production was a little boy, Robbie. He seems to be quite a character in his own right, working in hotels or catering establishments of some sort or other. As already mentioned, he was on Burgh Island, off Plymouth, for a while. Robbie seems to be a popular lad wherever he goes, which is a blessing.

The last of the Azopardi 'outfit' was Naomi. It is a great pity that she missed months, no, years, off her school education. Catching up with the aid of computers helps but it is not the same as going to school.

Unfortunately John 'Azo' has had years and years of illness.

He came from Gibraltar and can speak Spanish fluently. Jeyne has been over there several times visiting his family, and of course, she was very interested in the Rock and the Barbary Apes. It was one of that tribe which bit Grandma's sister, Auntie Young, when she was living there with her father, a military man stationed on 'The Rock'. It was thought to be the cause of her death many years later because of some unforeseen complications.

Jeyne and John now live at Horsham but ill as he is John wants to move home, preferably ending his days in the West Country. Naomi was thinking of trying to get into Plymouth University if they found a property near enough.

I have a telephone conversation with Jeyne every Friday about 2pm. Sometimes we can manage a visit – always a pleasure.

Offspring number two was John David, always a quiet gentle child. He worked hard with us here at Brookside until the M23 came too near and farming had to take a back seat – to use a queer expression.

He did some work locally but decided to give Surrey a miss altogether and went down to Devon and stayed with Mrs Williams at Starcross and worked on road construction. But during harvest time he went back to farming, working with an agency, and ended up in Yorkshire.

He liked Yorkshire, and there he met a young lady Sue – and that began the usual pattern of setting up home. I visited them once, when young Daniel was a toddler. Of Emily, his sister, I know very little and only what I can gather from the school photographs and the most recent ones would suggest that she is no longer a schoolgirl but has become a very attractive blonde. John has a job which means quite a long car journey every day, Sue helps – or did for many years – with school dinners.

For years they would not consider giving a dog a home, but I believe there is now a canine member of the family – Daniel and John doing most of the 'walkies'!

Daniel works in a newsagent's shop and 'split hours' mean that he has to start very early. He came down here with his dad after Christmas and I would say that he is a very nice lad.

My 'last chick' was – is – Janet and she now lives with me since Douglas died. It was felt that I needed more protection than one dog and a chained gate could provide, especially after I found

113

the gate open on two occasions and part of a motor mudguard resting on the garden path, so it was arranged that she would come to live with me with her little dog 'Bryn' and her nine cats. They are well housed – because of the road and its speeding monsters they had to be permanent tenants – and they are up in a shed for which I paid to be adapted securely. They have two rooms, a passage and an outdoor run – the latter popular in good weather.

Her Lucy – now working in Scotland – and James in the Army, have been able to visit us, always a pleasure for me.

Janet has done all sorts of work to improve living conditions generally. She decided the pear tree was not safe and I am afraid that John (Yorkshire) confirmed this.

So, of course, the pear tree had to come down. Janet thought one particular branch was most dangerous so she investigated, brought some height assistance – I've forgotten just what – and started sawing. Before there was any chance of the limb falling down I was presented with a yellow coat for protection and requested to stand out in the road to warn traffic. The 'yellow thing' was scarcely big enough so I felt a little like a sausage bursting out of its skin! The branch came down satisfactorily and the remainder of the tree was eventually dealt with by men.

Her car was standing out 'in the weather' – not the best treatment for a vehicle which you want to start easily and go. One day I had an idea, I thought there was just enough space for a shelter up behind Douglas's garage, so I investigated. Now, after quite a lot of hard work on the part of several people, a sufficient shelter exists and the car goes in and out satisfactorily.

The garden soon became the incinerator area and all sorts of things, big and small, met their fate on the pile of sticks down the path. Yes, there have been some good bonfires.

All round the garden there had been a growth of the roses which Douglas had planted some years ago. I know they should have been trimmed last year – now they have been and I am looking forward to whatever they can produce this year.

Out in the field, up in the corner right near to the aerodrome buildings, there is an overgrowth of nettles. I mentioned recently that I thought we ought to get that area treated with weed-killer. No, no, no! It must be dealt with in any other way but not weed-killer! I can see somebody spending hours and hours up in that corner in the spring and summer. I think that the most appropriate 'first-aid' tool will be a hook!

Janet has even been busy on the back lawn. To start with there were ants' hills which had to be levelled and treated. Then, above what must have been a well supplying 'the other cottage' the area has been properly levelled and light coloured bricks (a gift) make a platform for several kinds of pot plants. They were very attractive in the autumn, but don't ask me what they are called, I never remember!

The 'delicate' plants are resting in their pots up in the hay and no doubt between long walks for 'Girlie' and 'Bryn' they will be brought back to grace the garden still further.

Yes, Janet has been very busy.

28

Brookside Now

Gypsy the pony must be well over 20 years old, as tame as a kitten. One of her greatest delights is to roll in wet grass, muddy grass, she does not mind. She also stands out in the rain – by her own choice in spite of having plenty of cover.

Then there is that other animal – Girlie, a canine with the sweetest of natures. I'm afraid that she cannot be allowed to run free in case she chases a rabbit out on to the road. We have had a plague of them and some say that they are not afraid of man – or his dog – but she has managed to catch quite a number in spite of the long lead. There are some sheds still with some straw in them and at times they become the shelter for 'Mum Rabbit' until Girlie finds them.

A few years back two black and white cats seemed to find us – our own 'Blackie' was quite old and I cannot decide whether he welcomed these strangers or not. One cat was bigger than the other, and with only half an ear – older too and more mature than the slimmer animal. They were not here all the time, seemed to judge when to come so as not to meet the dog coming round the corner.

In the past, when I went out milking Dorcas every morning, I would take railed oats and nuts and sugar beet – and there he was again – a cheeky little robin redbreast. He waited for me to put the cow's food into her bucket and if I as much as dropped an oat Little Robin picked it up. So you know what happened! I put a crop full on top of a bin lid and Little Robin was not slow to take my offerings.

Crab Hill Lane used to be quiet with a few cars morning and evening and some in the day, too, of course. Now, if you want to take a car out of the drive in the mornings or evenings it is almost a hazardous experience, you might have to wait quite a few minutes. I am afraid that it will only get worse as the council give planning permission for more and more houses in the South East.

It is a pity not more use can be made of the system of 'tied' cottages where a house went with the work there. The amount of traffic could be cut, too, but I do not suppose any one will listen to me.

Brookside has been my home ever since 1955 and as I look around I can find many things, big and little, which remind me of Bremridge.

For instance there is a large oak tree just up on our boundary. It is very old and some of the topmost branches have been 'weathered away' in the storms over the years. That hedge 'catches' the wind from the broad expanse of the aerodrome and it does it no good.

The oak tree on Bremridge hill on the way to or from school was probably just as old, maybe even older, but it had been struck by lightning so that the top portion sprouted naked arms held up to the sky. But, as children, we were more interested in the roots because they seemed to come out at just the right place to make the arms of a chair. The lane, then, was rough and stony, but the view was good; you could sit and see who was going – or coming on Cross Hill.

Our present, Brookside, Oak Tree used to provide a good look-out just above its sturdy stump. In fact the children constructed a platform inviting periods of rest from whatever they had been doing around the outhouses with their occupants of different species.

Our land here slopes to the south and at the bottom of the field there is a stream – not one to be paddled in, though, most of it is a little too deep for that.

At Bremridge, the Holly Water which was named by a Devonshire lady as 'The Holy Water', borders several fields, in some places very deep and cattle have been known to have lost their lives in it.

Then there are the views – only at Brookside one has to go to Top Nutfield to appreciate the distances, the different areas, some wooded, some grazing, some cultivated.

A walk up to Hellions Down, Prestown Down or Wedgycleeve in Devon would provide far distant scenes. Sometimes, too, you could hear 'the guns on Dartmoor'. In another direction there was an awareness of life, traffic, etc., in the City of Exeter, and I am actually old enough to remember riding in a horse-drawn cab to, or from, Crediton Station, and I am sure it was in the period when Auntie Alma was ill in Bristol. She died there, aged 26.

Birds seem to be fairly common to both places, particularly little robins, tits, etc. I always seem to find another little robin here as soon as one disappears or is just a bundle of feathers. Up on what we always have called 'the long house' there appears to be an owl with diarrhoea according to the messes on the floor which have just missed the hay!

29

Some Lessons in Life

Bird Song

It was a cold and frosty morning, quite chilly. One of those mornings when every bit of metal you touched seemed to bite at your fingers. Gloves were certainly needed but this morning they had been left on top of a feed bag in the 'First House'.

The morning chores must be done however grim the world looked with frost on the grass and no sign of the sun. That may come later.

Everything was very quiet – until the little bird sang. Lovely little notes of sweet music came from its little feathered throat and it was so near I thought if I reach up I could almost touch it. I did not try. I let it sing on and enjoyed its little song, but now the world seems a better place if such a little bird can find something to sing about.

No socks, no boots, no hat or coat, how could he be so cheerful?

The Leaf and the Chestnut Tree

In the hedge opposite our gate there was something which fascinated me and made me wonder, as I often do, at the complexities of nature, for it was one particular leaf which could not keep still. It was growing on a horse chestnut tree which in terms of ages of such trees I suppose was fairly young, but I had watched it growing from a small sapling to the strong and tall specimen it had now become. The leaves, all of them, were strong and bright and green but there was one leaf which was in constant movement even if there was little – or no – breeze. It wagged and fluttered apparently unable to keep still, almost as if it was talking and had *very* much to say. Why just this one leaf?

The tree was really growing above a waterway – a gutter which did not often carry water unless there had been a downpour! The usual gutter weeds became abundant in the summer and made a safe look-out for the four-legged two eared pest – the rabbit.

Squirrels

Yes, these 'charming' little animals have teeth as sharp as razors and a climbing ability second to none. I have suffered many broken rolled oat sacks at the 'hands' of 'bushy-tail'. I used to enjoy seeing them in the big oak trees opposite but not any more after the way they waste and destroy food meant for other animals. However carefully I cover supplies, still there is a little gnawed hole and 'other evidence' which could not have been part of a bird – or rat.

The Complaint of Two Crows

If there is such a thing as a Court of Justice for Birds I know I would be reported and have to answer a charge of favouritism! Who can blame me for having a gentleman who was always pleased to see me and who awaited my visits with impatience?

I'd better tell you the whole story and then you can be the Judge!

It all began when two black gentlemen thought they had discovered a wonderful source of luxury food – titbits for the cow or something for the fowls – and they investigated the contents of the little plastic bags awaiting delivery to their rightful destinations. I lost bag and all one day as I was not in time to stop it being lifted all the way up to the roof of a shed. There the contents were disposed of quite quickly and the bag blew about in the wind.

The two black coated gentlemen were nowhere to be seen as I set out to do the feeding, but they seemed to know the time and would be sitting on any roof-top or post or any high point which would give them a view.

I won on this particular morning – and I would continue

winning every other day too, and I thought they would be very cross. I put the luxuries in a deep bucket and I put a lid on the top which I hoped they would be unable to remove. They could not shift it.

They still kept a very sharp watch and they squawked loudly.

The other gentleman who was so pleased to see me was a kind and considerate little being – he also waited for something to eat. He did not demand but walked just in front of me, looking back to see if I was coming, and even if the cat was there it did not frighten him away. How could anyone ignore such a polite request? It also gave me time to study his beauty, his colourful head, the sheen on his feathers, the long tail almost marked off in inches!

So, if there is a place where the behaviour of humans is discussed by birds my little pheasant friend would put on his glasses, look at his notes, and say something in my favour.

The other two, each in his turn, would thump the table loudly and shout a list of my sins demanding that I should be 'squawked at' morning and night and at any other time of the day when I might appear out of doors, whether carrying food or not.

I would receive support from the thousands of little birds, robins, sparrows and tits which abound by the poultry shed, often, I am afraid, sampling the food not actually meant for them!

Descendant of Brer Rabbit

There was a rabbit sitting on the lawn in the sun. No, not in the evening just before dark, this was in broad daylight and in spite of everything he, or she, had been there for quite a little while. Brer Rabbit's offspring was quite unconcerned about the cars passing up and down the road, not worried about the planes which gently glided in or roared out up over the trees and was, apparently, unaware that there was a big black cat lurking around the buildings. Not only that, there was a stray cat which had been around for some time and I am sure that animal would have been only too pleased to have rabbit pie – and would not bother whether it was cooked or raw!

One car was not just going up the road – it was making more noise than usual, 'scorching' we used to call it – and that did send Bunny back off the grass and under the shelter of the rose hedge.

j

Brer Rabbit Junior came out again when danger had passed.

So, in fact, rabbits have surmounted many hazards in their furry existence, they have beaten all man's efforts so far to eliminate them from the face of the earth. See what a plague they became in Australia and no doubt still are in some parts of that vast land. The man with a gun has succeeded in securing many 'for the cooking pot' until that terrible disease myxomatosis wiped out millions – but still they have come back.

Bit like us humans, actually, whatever wars and famines there are, whatever floods, earthquakes, accidents on the road, the rail, yes, and in the air, however horrible we are to each other, there are still plenty of us left – to breed like rabbits!

I quite liked to see Bunny on the lawn.

An Unusual Sound

I was busy one morning about my usual tasks down in the farmyard when I heard a most unusual sound. It sounded like a dog barking, but we did not have a dog and I looked all round the buildings and there was nothing. Then I thought 'my cow cannot bark, and the pony cannot, so, perhaps, it was the cat', but puss was there, sitting down quite happily and waiting for her share of something nice to drink – yes, milk – for she always has her little green bowl filled every morning. Then she clears off somewhere to sleep for the rest of the day.

Several days later I saw something in the field which could explain the mystery – a black dog obviously on the lookout for rabbits, and there had been plenty of them in this district at that time! Black dog was accompanied by another animal not much bigger than a rabbit, but a proper 'little scruff'.

They went, but they returned several times and the little one was obviously too afraid of people to allow you to say anything to it, to ask it where it came from, or anything else. The big one belonged to the greyhound/whippet breed and was the thinnest thing on four long legs that I had seen for years.

When I went to fetch a bale of straw for bedding for the night for Dorcas and Gypsy I was more than surprised to see a long black shape spring up and disappear beyond the nearest hedge. Yes, you've guessed it – it was the big black dog, and I wished that I had some food for her. I hoped she would come back and continue her sleep for I had no wish to turn her out.

Next day I did leave some food out and soon it was gone. Next day I did the same and there it was – gone again or, rather, not there.

Little scruff seemed to have disappeared completely, but you can guess where the big black dog was, and being well fed. We called her 'Girlie' – living in the straw, eating rabbits and the scraps. There seemed to be many more scraps now that the cow, the pony and the fowls would not eat, but they had a very ready market via a thin black dog with her head on one side and her long tawny legs ready to run away.

To Rock a Rook or Cradle a Crow!

Big black birds abound in spring in the area where I live, but I never could tell a rook from a crow! They must all belong to the same family of opportunists taking their chance to pick up anything, and everything, they fancy. Often in the garden, often in a field looking for any speck which might be termed food, I suppose they could be doing good by clearing harmful insects or scavenging what some other animal has left behind.

I had noticed a construction – a thing which from a distance looked like a large football – built into the high branches of a tall tree. I had noticed this tree swaying in the wind but the 'football' stayed put. Of course it was clever of the nest builders to select such a site for it was safe from several risks which other nest builders faced; no cat could climb up there, no fox could reach, and even an agile squirrel would be hard pressed to climb up those small branches, swaying in the wind. If the birds had chosen an oak, the nest would not have moved in the wind, so there would be more danger of the sticks, the building material, being blown away, for in the winds which we had been experiencing at the time something had to give!

I wonder who chooses the nest site – does 'Mr' Rook (or Crow) say, "Here we are, Missus, we won't get a better place than this, so start collecting." Perhaps 'Mrs' Crow (or Rook) mutters about it being the ideal site for her to lay her eggs in and encourages the 'Mr' of the species to gather the necessary material. Whoever it was, they both worked hard together and the construction was safe for the hen and the eggs and the baby birds

123

when they were hatched.

I watched the parents visiting the nest. It was quite windy and by the frequent trips I was sure they were feeding young, so it was certainly a case of 'Rock-a-bye baby on the tree top, when the wind blows the cradle will rock,' but there was little chance of the bough breaking – the cradle to rock a rook or comfort a crow had been very well constructed!

'Mr Squire' and The Squirrels

In the little bit of Surrey seen from my windows the hedges along by the road had not been trimmed for many years and they did not resemble the neat cut appearance of the fields belonging to the modern farmer with his big hedge trimming machine. There were several large oak trees with enough scrub growth between them to form a perfect pathway for squirrels to have their own traffic system but from the ground who could say how many little furry bodies there were to jump or swing from one branch to another? One squirrel looks so much like his neighbour and behaves in much the same way that unless you see them together you just do not know.

So, I was lucky one day – dreaming out of the window for a few minutes with nothing more to do than to enjoy the January air, when I saw one coming from the furthest oak all along over the scrub right up through the nearest tree and on to somewhere else. He, or she, looked just like someone off shopping – you know, in a hurry and with somewhere to go. I saw squirrel go back again in a few minutes, mission accomplished.

For a few seconds longer I tarried, idly, and then I saw something very interesting. What I thought was the stump of a branch cut off after the 1987 storms began to move, it began to scratch its ear, to preen itself! Then on another branch a furry tail began to move and a little body jumped forward, so there were three, and they 'made tracks' and disappeared like magic, for a bigger older squirrel had appeared! Mr Squire, protector, schoolmaster, lover, or what? Obviously it was not wise to hang around in the same tree, so I assume that the little squirrels knew their place!

My Two-wheeled Trolley and Four-wheeled Truck

My two-wheeled trolley came into my possession in the early '70s. It was painted green and had a removable body over its wooden platform. With its two good wheels it balanced quite nicely when it was loaded.

Long, long before I owned it the two-wheeled trolley or truck, same thing – began life on a railway station where it must have seen many comings and goings, probably back as far as the 1914/18 war. Who knows what tales it could have told of partings and meetings, etc., if only it had been able to speak.

It would have been loaded with all sorts of luggage; smart cases, rucksacks and bags of all descriptions which the anxious owners were only too ready to retrieve. It could have carried the luggage of people going on holiday and coming home again with some strange looking bags and parcels.

Eventually there came a time when it was pensioned off by the stationmaster and either sold – or given – to some odd-job man who could make good use of it. He made sides and top and bottom ends and it became a little truck in use for years.

Then the old man retired and the trolley came my way for use on a very small farm. It carried hay bales and poultry and cow feeding stuffs and bags of manure. It was a most useful little truck – until the sides wore out and the platform had to be renewed. It also had to receive a new pair of wheels, so it became a flat bottomed trolley and continued a very useful life.

One day, and I have the exact date 6/9/96, it could not be found. It had been stolen. I looked round for something to replace it and found a smaller vehicle which had actually started life as a pushchair for a child. It had four wheels and certain alterations had to be carried out before a good-sized box did duty for carrying my farming paraphernalia. It had been extremely useful but I could not expect it would last forever and eventually saw where the strain was affecting the wheels, they were beginning to buckle.

I have actually worn out three perambulators, mainly gifts but one I did buy at a jumble sale up in the village, so, really, going up and down the garden path with their burdens did not do them much good!

The Sharp Little Birdie

I know I have mentioned birds before, but this one is special – she is just like Mrs Billinghurst.

Who was Mrs Billinghurst? She was a lady I knew years ago – a sharp, quick little lady with a fresh complexion and very controlled fairish hair, almost a ginger, straight, of course, for people in those days – my youth – were not bothered about getting it permed, that fashion came later. She wore lozenge-shaped gold spectacles which often slipped half way down over her nose and she would poke them back up again with a very slim finger. Her movements were always quick – they did not have time to be graceful.

So who could be like her, who could bridge all the years between then and now and bring back such a personality?

No one except a little sparrow, a hen sparrow alighting on the top rail of a fence and starting to clean her beak by wiping it this way and that across the sharp edge of the top rail. There was a pause during which she looked around making sure of her space, her position, with no one to disturb her. Then she continued her 'this way and that' movement as she was not satisfied that she was spotless.

What had she been eating I wondered? Perhaps she had picked something off the roses, perhaps she had discovered a large juicy caterpillar. Maybe she had needed to dig in the earth before the prize was hers. At last she seemed satisfied and flew off, her tiny wings carrying her up on to a branch of the nearest tree. I lost sight of her then and I thought to myself if she reappears I shall christen her 'Mrs Billinghurst'.

She did not come back, but one year we had a host of small birds which found apples on our few apple trees very much to their liking. I made jam with as many apples as I could but very much regretted that the birds could be so destructive – or greedy! They alighted on the branches of the trees and pecked every apple in sight – it was our worst invasion by birds.

Of course, the next plague was the furry bunny for 'Buck' and his wives and sisters seemed to find the pears under the large old tree in the corner of the lawn very much to their liking. Perhaps they said to themselves, "She's coming again, bite 'em up quickly, boys!"

Rabbits

I must have had rabbits on my mind – there were so many of them running about. They seemed to be everywhere, down under the apple trees waiting for every apple which dropped, running across the fields, even on the front lawn where they were trying to help by cutting the grass. Sometimes they sat very quiet and still and so resembled a stone or piece of wood but no stone or lump of wood scampers away showing a little white tail.

Therefore it was not surprising that I dreamed about the little creatures one night – as follows:

A perfectly ordinary half-grown bunny spoke to me as I was walking down the garden path. He came out from behind a rose bush, looked at me and did not run away. He lowered his right ear and lifted his right hind leg, almost as if he was making a salute.

"M'am," he said, "can I speak to you for a few minutes?" The voice sounded a little husky, but the words were clear enough.

"I'm listening," I said. "What do you want?" He made the same dropped ear hind leg salute again, so I said, "Why do you do that?"

He replied, "Well, M'am, my Great Grandfather said that all rabbits had to be respectful when speaking to a member of the 'Two-leg Gang' and you are one of them so I am trying to show respect."

"What was your Great Grandfather's name?" I asked.

Salute again! Perhaps it was at the thought of his Great Grandfather, obviously remembered very well. Then he said, "Please M'am, it was Buck and my Grandfather was William, and my Dad was John."

"What are you called?"

There was another hind leg salute, and almost a bow before he answered, "Me, M'am, I'm Chopper."

"Well, Chopper," I said, "what do you want? I'm listening, and you have shown respect so you can stop saluting me now." The last time he had done it he had nearly lost his balance and I thought he was going to fall over, but he had quickly recovered.

"Can you get rid of that big black cat because I am sure he caught my sister the other day and I know she will never come back home to us again. You, M'am, you cut down all the lovely

127

tall weeds in the field so now we have only got the hedge to hide in and we have to have a 'Guard Rabbit' in case a fox is looking for one of us. I had a young cousin – very pretty young thing, I was going to marry her myself when she was old enough – but a fox caught her so she is another who will never come back."

"Well, Chopper, the weeds had to go – after all, you had them for quite a long time, and as for cats and foxes you will just have to watch out and be very careful. I'm sorry I cannot help."

"Thank you, M'am," he said. He hopped off and gave another salute but this time it was quite different for I am sure that I saw him lifting his hind leg from his twitching little nose!

Life's Like That

In a country village there are nearly always people you know when you visit the doctor's surgery. It is always a friendly place and most people speak to their companions who are also waiting to see the doctor. Sometimes it can be quite a long wait and you do not know how many there are in front of you with difficult and time-consuming problems.

So it was quite natural for me to ask the plump lady who entered after me what had happened to her leg, very obviously heavily bandaged.

"I took all the skin off me shin," she said. "It was foretold to me that I should fall down and hurt my leg, but I didn't believe it."

Apparently a fortune teller had told her to be very careful because she could 'see an accident, a fall' and the plump lady said that she had been exceedingly careful out in the street, going everywhere slowly. She had almost crawled upstairs, and crawled down again. She had taken care at the railway station and down her own garden path – everywhere – until she opened her own French windows to shake a duster out and had fallen down the two concrete steps!

So the fortune teller was right!

A Silly Old Woman and a Naughty Cow

My Bess looked lovely. Her fine textured coat was that of a dark Jersey, her back was straight and her udder was well formed and well rounded for she was due to calve at any time. Of course I 'kept an eye' on her and this calf she was expecting would be her third production.

I had not bought Bess, nor was she a gift. I had exchanged her for 'Garbo', a cow who had been so correctly named it was almost unbelievable! She had been all right when I was the only person around – I could get her in for milking without any difficulty, but let the AI man or the vet have need to come near her and she was gone – gone over the gate and down the field, and when the young girl from the ministry came to do the brucellosis test Garbo said most definitely, "I vent to be alone," and the lady had to arrange to come creeping up behind her when she was routinely in for milking!

Therefore, when a neighbouring young farmer said he would take her into his herd which was complete with a bull and I could have a 'little Jersey' instead, I agreed.

So Garbo, with several young companions, went to a new home. Bess came here, in calf, with still a few months to wait after feeding her own last son or daughter, and she needed a rest from 'mothering' to recover condition.

Well, she produced her third calf without any problem, a lovely little Charolais heifer, and then the trouble started. Bess turned her head round, lifted a hind leg and quite easily began to milk herself!

I thought back. Her previous owner had said, "I think she had a sore on a front teat at one time – all right now, though."

One way of dealing with the problem would be to keep her permanently 'tied', as often happens in winter anyway when cows are lying in. But this was summer and glorious weather – so that method was out. She was well able to feed two calves and another was provided for her. I hoped that her mothering instinct would be strong enough to overcome her own desire for milk; it was not, so I had to think again.

I did ask for advice from someone who had kept cows all his life – and knew 'everything' about them! This gentleman, smoking his pipe, and looking wise, said, "You'll never do aught with her, missus. Put her back in market."

Not without a jolly good try to stop her, I thought.

About this time I had many black polythene sacks, and I thought it would be possible to make her a 'bra' by tying each end to a long piece of baler string and tying it up over her back so that it did, indeed, make a bra!

It worked – until she went out in the field, where the artful monkey deliberately walked under the bough of an overhanging tree, leaving bra on the ground!

"Put a thing in her nose – that'll stop her," said her previous owner when I informed him of the situation. "I'll come up and put it in for you." So the 'horrible thing' – an anti-sucking plate – was acquired and, true to his word, he did what was necessary. But it did not stop her.

All this time, of course, Bess only went in to feed her calves and was turned out again when they had had enough. Before she left their little house I got busy with a large cake of soap – all round her teats and udder.

Kitchen soap did not stop her – she seemed to like the taste. I tried a highly scented 'lady's soap' and this lasted a little longer but she did become used to the smell and, although it showed that smells or scents might ultimately be the answer to stopping her 'self-milking', I should have to find something a little more obnoxious!

By using a plastic bag, which had contained nothing more sinister than a loaf of bread, one morning it was even possible for me to use this as a glove and smother her beautiful udder in 'loose' dung after she had fed her calves. By feeding time some of it had disappeared and I had to wash the rest off ready for the calves to have their supper!

Not for a moment did I think that Bess and I would remain at loggerheads for ever. Somewhere there must be something which would keep her 'off' but the 'anti-sucking plate' in her nose was not the answer. Apparently it is not unknown for a cow to have this vice but I certainly would not adopt the method advocated by someone who obviously had experience of it – to put barbed wire round 'the thing'!

The Ministry of Agriculture 'ordained' (as my Grandfather would have said) that our own vet should come to test the cattle for brucellosis, and after he had finished his part of the job I told him of my problem with Bess and of what I thought of using on her udder.

"Would it hurt her?" I asked. "Even if I had to use it over a longish period?"

He thought not, but I did not think I would follow his suggestion of 'trying it on myself'!

130

So, I bought myself a large bottle of antiseptic. I offered it to her to smell – and her head turned away like a whip-top. I had to take her away from her calves, of course, milk her myself and feed them by bucket – no problem, anyway, as they were beginning to have too much and 'too much' for youngish calves could lead to a considerable amount of trouble.

After every milking I was fairly liberal with the antiseptic, all round her sides near her udder, on the 'bag' itself, but I did avoid her teats.

It stopped her milking herself. She has now had another calf and is behaving just as she should so it does appear that I have won!

Perhaps I am not such a silly old woman after all!

Insects in the Garden

Flutter by, butterfly, what can you see?
Flutter by, butterfly, do not sit on me.

Red Admiral and Cabbage White, One so pretty, one so light:
Red Admiral and Cabbage White, now they're here, now out
of sight.

"Whizz, whizz" says Willie Wasp, "What can I sting?"
"Whizz, whizz," says Willie Wasp, "I must find something."

High, high, high overhead I can hear a bumble sing;
High, no, lower overhead, now I see the whirr of wing.

What is that on my nose? Oh, it's landed on my toes.
There it goes, miles away – "Fly, I'll catch you one day."

Ants, so many, so brown, where is your little town?
Ants, so many, so brown, you do cause many a frown.

Little grasses, big grasses, all are pushed down flat.
Little grasses, big grasses, there rolled that tabby cat!